This Book

Lucky Boy

THE STORY OF JOE LYNCH

Joseph D. Lynch & Corey Radman

Joseph D. Lynch/Lucky Boy
Printed in the United States of America

Lucky Boy/ Joseph D. Lynch. -- 1st ed.

ISBN Print 978-0-692-90343-8 Edition

ISBN Ebook 978-0-692-90344-5 Edition

Contents

To Terri, I Love You.
And to my grandkids and their parents, with my love.

"Any boy who has a mother who is totally dedicated to his success is a lucky boy."

Introduction

Think back with me. It's 1966. After seven long years of study, I'm about to graduate from Creighton University's School of Medicine in Omaha, and I'm not looking forward to it. To be clear, I'm looking forward to further training and practicing medicine; it's the graduation ceremony that has me shaking my head. In those years, Creighton's graduation ceremony combined all the professional degree programs along with the undergraduates into one grueling exercise in patience. All I could imagine was hours of sitting, waiting for the five seconds it would take me to walk across the stage and gather my diploma. Not worth the hassle, I was thinking.

Skipping was my plan until I talked to Pat, my sister, who was 18 years older than me—a second mother to me, really. She was excited for me. Wanting to plan for the day, she was full of questions. "When do you graduate? What day is it? Where will we need to go? Where is the celebration?"

I replied, "Well, I wouldn't worry about it. I might be able to get out of going to graduation..."

Due to transferring to Creighton after my third year as an undergraduate, I had managed to skip my graduation ceremony at Gonzaga University. I was hoping to do the same thing a second time. Pat paused for a long time. Her eyebrows furrowed. She pinned me down with a firm expression and said in that scathing way big sisters have,

"What are you talking about? This really doesn't have anything to do with you. It is for Mom."

Pat was right. In fact, graduation day did prove to be Mom's day. At age 70, life was a pretty serious endeavor for my mother, Cecilia Agnes O'Malley Lynch. She was an "all business" kind of woman. Often when we were out together, Mom would get annoyed because people would assume she was my grandmother. (Who could blame them for taking a look at her gray hair and leaping to that conclusion?) But that day, Mom was all smiles. She worked her way up the Civic Auditorium steps in her good church clothes, a coat and a hat, and sat there grinning the whole time. That smile helped me realize that Pat was right. This occasion was important to my mom, probably more important than it was to me. Seeing her pleasure helped me stop and enjoy the day as well.

Mom was never a woman to cry much, in public or private. That day was no different; there was no crying, but there was that great big grin. And one other thing—she hugged me.

Mom was not a hugger. Hugs were reserved for formal, important occasions, like the day I left for medical school. So, when I found her in the crowd and showed her my diploma, she grabbed me and squeezed. "Proud of you, Joe," she said. I wasn't expecting a hug, so it was awkward for us both. It probably looked like someone trying to embrace a coat hanger. But the singularity of the hug showed again how pleased and how proud she was of me. In a way, the accomplishment of medical school was hers. She sacrificed a lot to get me there.

And it wasn't easy. Mom raised me on her own. Pat was much older, already out of high school and starting college by the time I was born. And my dad died three days after my sixth birthday. So, you can't talk about me growing up without also telling the story of my mother. It was just the two of us.

Chapter 1

How We Got Here

I – Philip Wilfred Lynch, Paternal Grandfather

There is hope in the sea but none in the land.
(Irish proverb)

Across the ocean, they came, the many strands of the Irish diaspora. Forced off the land, barely educated, without a trade and fleeing the famines, they came To America.

From County Longford, from Sligo, Roscommon, Down, Kilkenny and from Liverpool, they came.

To New York and Boston, to Pennsylvania, Illinois, Iowa and Nebraska, they came. They prayed, they protested and they rioted.

They were laborers and maids, dockworkers, blacksmiths, and well drillers. They worked in the mines and steel mills. They founded and filled the bars and the churches.

They died on both sides of the Civil War. It was the 8th Ohio and the 69th Pennsylvania, flying the colors of both the Union and of Ireland, who held the point on cemetery ridge against Pickett's Charge at Gettysburg.

They worked for the Union Pacific, the Burlington and the Denver and Rio Grande railroads.

They taught in the schools and founded universities.

They homesteaded the land. They married and had children.

O'Malleys married O'Malleys and Fitzgeralds. Lynches married McDermotts and McDowells. There were Flanagans and Graces, Brennans, Potters, Jordans and Sweeneys, as well Ryans, Fagans, Powers, Hughes, McFaddens, Liebharts, DeBackers, and more O'Malleys.

Theirs was the immigrant's dream, a decent job, a better life, some respect.

~Joseph Lynch

Like most people in the United States, I (Joseph Lynch) am descended from people who weren't born in this country. Some families are fairly separated from that history. So many generations have passed that the family memory gets a bit lost. That's not how it is in my family. For me, those Irish roots are very strong. Though more than 100 years have passed, only two generations separate me from those Irish immigrants.

We'll get back to my story soon, but if you want to understand me, you need to meet my predecessors. I am third-generation, American born and proud of it. As the verse above indicates, emotionally, in many ways, I am still an Irishman. My forefathers in this country were nearly all Irish immigrants. In fact, I once went to Galway, Ireland for a professional meeting. One of my colleagues went to introduce me to the Dean of the Galway Medical School. Though we had never met, he said, "Oh I know who Dr. Lynch is. He has the map of Ireland written on his face." I was pleased to be recognized by my genetics. Lynch is one of the original 14 tribes of Galway and is the most common surname in Galway; however, I have not been able to identify any members of my family from there.

I am proud of the contributions my family members made to this country. They were laborers, professionals, farmers, and soldiers. They were a part of the first big wave of immigrants who built America. All of those people had a hand in who I became, but one family member in particular has had a great deal of influence on where I landed and who I grew up to be. That is my paternal grandfather, Philip Wilfred Lynch. Let's call him Philip.

The father of my father, Philip was the man who brought the Lynch family line to Nebraska. Because the Lynches are long-lived, there are 100 years of United States history—but only two generations—between his birth and mine. That's from a combination of long lives and women who were able to have children in their forties. Philip was in the middle of most of my family-history stories. A durable man, he was born in 1858 and lived until the age of 79 when he died in 1938, four years before I was born.

Philip grew up in New York, the fourth child of an Irish immigrant. His father, Patrick Lynch, was from County Longford. He was initially a blacksmith in the Brooklyn Navy Yard but soon became a farmer in Oswego County, New York. Philip's childhood included schooling and helping out on the family farm. At 16, Philip left school and was entrusted with driving one of his father's teams of horses. Every winter, he hauled hemlock bark and hides to a tannery for leather making. (The bark was plopped into a soaking vat with the hardened hides to soften them before tanning.) Summers were devoted to farming.

At age 20, Philip decided to seek his fortune in the American west. In 1879, he filed a timber claim in Nebraska (according to the Timber Culture Act of 1873), but then decided to try silver mining in Leadville, Colorado. This was a tumultuous time in those boom and bust mining communities. Picture a town full of young, single men with fistfuls of cash. Philip was a devout Catholic. That wasn't the life he wanted. After four years of trying his hand at mining and then working as a mason for the Denver and Rio Grande Railroad, he gave it up and returned to Custer County, Nebraska, where the pace of life resembled the one he had grown up with—the one he wanted for himself and his future family. Philip returned to his timber claim and began preparing the land for farming. The Timber Culture Act granted claimants 160 acres of free land if they planted and nurtured trees on 40 acres of the land. It was an attempt to get more trees growing on the plains. It was felt this would preserve the topsoil and improve farming.

On that land, my grandfather built a house made of sod. (See photo in photo section.) In frontier-era Nebraska there was a LOT of prairie grass. By cutting blocks of soil bound tightly together by the dense, deep root system, homesteaders were able to create building supplies from nothing but the ground beneath their feet. The blocks stacked on top of one another to build walls. Inside, walls could be plastered and regular windows and doors fitted into the walls for the appearance of a finished home. It was probably a little damp in there, but compared to the alternative—nothing—I think it was a genius solution.

Looking at the photo from the outside, the house appears to have one large room with space for sleeping on one side and sitting/eating on the other. From the center of the house rises a chimney, which tells me that there was a wood stove that they would have used for cooking and heating the house.

At age 29 in 1887, Philip married my grandmother, Catherine Veronica McDowell, and they moved into that sod home in Custer County in an area called Lee's Park. Together they had six children, including my father, Patrick Francis Chester Lynch (born February 24, 1892). Five of those six children survived to adulthood. The Lynch family children included: Philip Leo, Patrick Francis Chester

(Dad), Bernard Urban (who died at age one), Ignatius McDowell, Katherine Veronica (who later became a Dominican order nun and took the name Sister Marceline), and James Joseph. Those kids were born, on average, about every two years between 1889 and 1901. It must have been awfully cozy in that sod house!

That probably explains why Philip sold that first plot and home in 1902 and moved to 620 acres of land that he purchased from the railroad on Buffalo Creek, five miles south of Oconto, Nebraska. The wood-frame home he built there was much larger; the family came to call it the "big house." (See photo in photo section.) That wood home was a huge step up from the sod house. Grand in scale and design, the rooms of that home hosted growing children, family gatherings, and aging parents. It remained a touchstone for the Lynch family until economic misfortune intervened. We'll get to that story soon enough.

Through the years, Philip not only farmed, but also raised cattle. Ultimately Philip had 225 acres under cultivation. He raised Shorthorn cattle and Poland-China hogs. Histories written about Custer County, Nebraska describe Philip as "one of Custer County's substantial men and dependable citizens." Though he was well respected, he never accepted offers to run for county leadership. Philip was very active in the Catholic church there.

My grandmother Catherine was of Irish ancestry, but she was born in Lincolnshire, England in 1864. She immigrated to Pennsylvania at age 7, but I wonder if an English sense of propriety lingered. As a wife and mother, she took pains to have things just right. In the "big house," she created a lovely home, and she loved to entertain frequently. The big house was the gathering spot for weekly Sunday dinner after Mass, complete with white linen tablecloths and cloth napkins. Father Moynihan from Oconto had a regular invitation to join them, along with many of the area Lynch family relations.

When she was elderly, my mother, Cecilia, confided that she considered the Lynches' Sunday white linen service to be a bit over the top for a ranch house. "They seem to think rather well of themselves," she murmured. I tried to take Mom's criticisms of Lynch customs with a grain of salt. She was an O'Malley, and that particular loaded comment is part of a story for later. I don't think my mom was off the mark in her opinion, however. Apparently, the Lynch family even had their own baseball team, complete with full uniforms, which for early 1900s Nebraska was pretty la-dee-da—especially for a cattle rancher.

But perhaps Catherine can be forgiven for trying to bring some big-city notions to the prairie. She not only originated in England, her parents were related to highly influential Irish Catholics in New York. Catherine's mother, Mary Hughes (my great-grandmother), was the niece of Archbishop John Hughes of New York. This man was the first archbishop of New York, the builder of St. Patrick's Cathedral, the founder of the Catholic education system in the United States, and the founder of Fordham University. Archbishop Hughes was a moral and civic leader, a highly influential man; he even served as an advisor to Abraham Lincoln on the matter of hospital chaplains.

Archbishop Hughes was also known as a bit of a tyrant. That may be so, but if he was, he was "our tyrant," aiding the nearly defenseless immigrants against those who despised them. Some said he was only interested in the Irish, and a shrewd (maybe even ruthless) adversary who would not be beaten. He came to be called Dagger John, which was a reference to the cross that accompanied his signature as well as a reminder that he was not a man to be double-crossed.

He was an American patriot and he had a well-documented generous and gentle side, especially with the poor. However, he also had numerous public debates and disagreements, usually with members of the established hierarchy of the city but also with leaders of some churches (including Roman Catholic)—both in Philadelphia (where he was Bishop prior to becoming Archbishop of New York) and New York City. There is no doubt that he was primarily focused on the Irish immigrants. Between 1845 and 1850, nearly one million of the "famine Irish" left their homeland, mostly headed for America, especially New York. Another million died in Ireland, out of an estimated total population of 8 to 9 million. The Irish were the first large group of poor immigrants to come to America. The hostility was massive and widespread. Archbishop Hughes meant to educate and to elevate both the American citizenry and the Irish immigrants.

Sometimes I wonder if Catherine's childhood associations with her famous great-uncle, Dagger John, and her influential family members in New York, might have made it difficult to be a farmer's wife in Nebraska. Though her husband did become influential and well respected in their region, she grew cantankerous in her later years. According to my mother, Cecilia, dealings with Catherine were often difficult, harsh even.

My father, Patrick Francis Chester Lynch, was the second child born to Philip and Catherine. He was born in 1892 in Arcadia, Nebraska. His initial schooling was primarily at home. His high school education was rather erratic in that he intermittently attended Lexington High School, twenty miles south of the Lynch homestead. Mom said he would go to Lexington in the fall to pick up books and assignments and return to Lexington in the spring. He was not able to attend school in the winter. He did graduate from Lexington High School in 1913, ranked first in his class of 22 students. Since he was valedictorian and also had two roles in the class play, he must have attended school more regularly at that time. His valedictory address was titled "Waste." I thought it was interesting that one of his two roles in the class play, "The Dear Boy Graduates," performed at the Smith Opera House in Lexington the night before graduation, was

Professor Hudson, the high school principal. He then went on to the Nebraska State Teachers College in Kearney, Nebraska that fall.

Though he had that long, distinguished name, mostly people just called him Chester. In fact, I didn't realize that it was one of his middle names until I started digging into family history. I always thought Chester was just a nickname. On his marriage license to my mom, he noted his name as Patrick F. C. Lynch. Because he passed away when I was barely six, I have far fewer of his stories and thoughts to pass along than I do of my mom's. That saddens me. And, it is a big reason why I set out to write this book. I want there to be a record for you, my family. I want any of you who are interested to have the opportunity to understand what I thought and did long after I am gone.

II – O'Malley Clan, My Maternal Grandparents

As I have alluded, my mother's side of the family came from more humble beginnings. The O'Malley ancestors emigrated from Ireland around the same era as the Lynches; however, their fortune on this continent wasn't as consistent or as lucrative. Many of my ancestors on both sides were famine Irish, immigrating in the 1840s and early 1850s, although a few appear to have immigrated as early as 1816 and as recent as the 1880s.

My maternal grandparents, William Anthony O'Malley and his wife, Mary Agnes Fitzgerald O'Malley, were both born in the Midwest in 1855 and 1858, respectively. They both were first-generation, American-born Irish and were apparently raised near Nokomis, Illinois. William and Mary married in 1880 and quickly started a family. They homesteaded a farm just north of Alda, Nebraska in the 1880s. Farming was very difficult, especially with drought and grasshoppers. They had ten children between 1881 and 1898. That's one child every two years. The ten children began with three boys: Michael, Peter, and Edward; then two girls: Margaret and Anna; numbers six and seven, William and Mary; the youngest three children, including my mother, were: Thomas, Cecilia, and redheaded John (called Jack). Jack and my mom were always close, probably owing to their shared time at the bottom of the family pecking order. In fact, as an adult, my mom would go on to help raise Jack's third child (Margaret, called Peg). More about that later. My mother's two oldest brothers, Mike and Peter, also grew to be important figures in my mom's life, but for very different reasons.

My grandfather, William O'Malley, the family patriarch, died unexpectedly at age 53, following the sudden onset of abdominal problems, possibly due to appendicitis. It was 1909. William Howard Taft had just been elected president. The wheat penny with Abraham Lincoln on the front made its debut. And my grandmother found herself alone on a Nebraska farm with ten children to manage. She was 51 years old.

Because the oldest son, Michael, was 28 years old, he stepped in to help fill his father's role. Together, Michael and my grandmother started a threshing business to help keep the family afloat. It was profitable enough to keep everyone fed. The trouble was that Michael, also called Mike, apparently could be a difficult person. My mother did not get along with him and found his efforts to "guide" her abrasive. Perhaps that was to be expected; Mom was 13 and probably didn't want to be parented by a mere brother. Mom also thought Mike drank too much (though, to be fair, she thought that everyone who consumed any amount of alcohol might have a problem). I did meet him when I was a child and thought he seemed awfully grouchy.

My memories of my Uncle Mike O'Malley also include his very kind wife, Aunt Katherine (Schulte). When I saw her she was always pleasant, always smiling...and completely deaf. I liked her a lot. When I asked my mother once who of those two relatives I was related to "by blood," my mother quipped, "I know why you are asking, and I am very sorry but it is Mike." Mike and Aunt Katherine's children and grandchildren grew up to be a wonderful family, which Mom attributed entirely to Aunt Katherine.

Things never got better between Mom and Mike. When their mother Mary died in 1929, Mike reportedly took the entirety of his mother's estate (without consulting any of the other siblings) and spent much of it on things he felt were important, like a good-sized O'Malley burial plot for the whole family in Grand Island. Cecilia and some of her siblings eventually sued Mike and won. That left Mom enough money to buy a house in Hastings, Nebraska in 1936.

As you read, keep in mind that these stories are pretty one-sided. I heard them from my mother and only have vague childhood memories to go on for first-person accounts. Mike O'Malley may not have been all that bad. He was once the youngest person ever elected to the Nebraska State Legislature (1913-15). So, he had something going for him. Of course, Mom said he made it on their dad's good name. Some grudges die hard.

Though Mom had a hard time with Mike, she was very close with the family's second son, Peter. As a young man, Peter moved to Washington State to work in a logging camp. He wrote her letters occasionally and sent the family the Sunday *Seattle Times* newspaper regularly, which she enjoyed revisiting years later when the two of us lived in the Pacific Northwest. I think having that connection to her well-loved and respected brother made her proud to be loved by and connected to such a kind person.

In a letter dated September 8, 1918, Peter wrote to my mom: "Dear Sister, Well, I guess I will drop a line to let you know that I am still among the living." He goes on to mention that the previous week, when he was away from camp, the logging operation "had a runaway and smashed the locomotive and three cars..." Two people were killed, etc. He ends the letter very affectionately. Not two months later, Peter was killed. According to a letter from one of Peter's co-workers, they thought of him as the superintendent on the job. The friend related that Peter actually had that day off but one of his employees had been ordered by a locomotive engineer to do something unfair ("an unjust demand, a manifest wrong"), and Peter, rather than making his employee do it, said he would do it himself, which tragically resulted in his death.

One amazing fact about the O'Malley family was that all those ten children survived until at least the age of 20...though that bit of good luck didn't mean the family was immune to tragedy. There were some incredibly tough years too. My mom was born in 1896, and her father died in 1909. Between 1913 and 1918 three of her brothers died (Peter, William, and Thomas). Additionally, two nieces and nephews died. Also, somewhere in there her brother, Edward, decided that he owned the Union Pacific Railroad and everyone was robbing him, which resulted in spending the rest of his life living in the state mental hospital. Mom once recalled the time to my sister, "In those years, all we were doing was going to funerals."

All this family sadness may have had something to do with my mom attending high school in Alton, Illinois at the Ursuline Academy for two years. Two of her aunts were nuns and teachers at the school. Perhaps completing her tenth- and eleventh-grade years there helped instill some stability in Cecilia's life. The Ursuline school functioned as a college preparatory institution, but according to family letters, Mom didn't love being away from home.

She completed her high school education at Grand Island High School, which was very close to her home near Alda, Nebraska. Mom was happy to be home again. She enjoyed socializing and loved to dance, especially at Shimmers Lake, which had a dance hall. It had a bar too, but Mom (and Dad) never drank. Mom said Dad "took the

Irish pledge not to drink alcohol when he was a teenager and always kept it."

After high school graduation, Mom taught in a one-room school (District 1, Hall County), which was on the road between Shimmers Lake and Alda. This allowed her to save some money. She attended summer school at the teachers college in Kearney in 1917 and '18 and went a full year in 1921-22.

III – Cecilia & Chester Lynch, My Parents

My sister, Pat, said Mom mentioned Dad courted her for three summers. He visited her and sent letters. They went dancing, and they also shared some time together at the college in Kearney. When Dad was 30 years old and Mom was 26, the two were married, on August 30, 1922 at St. Mary's Church in Grand Island, Hall County, Nebraska.

Dad got a job teaching school in the town of Heartwell, Nebraska, population 200. He was the school superintendent and coached the high school sports teams, as well as being one of the three teachers at the high school. He was a real one-man show, but he didn't mind. He really loved working with kids and the people of Heartwell. Mom taught there one year, 1923, but then she became pregnant and stayed home with their first child, Pat.

Their daughter, my sister Pat, was born at home on February 4, 1924 in Heartwell, Nebraska. When Pat was two years old, our cousin Margaret O'Malley (Peg), came to live with the family. Peg was the daughter of Jack O'Malley (Cecilia's brother) and Agnes Clayes O'Malley. Agnes died when Peg was ten months old. Peg's two other siblings, Jim and Bill, were older and were sent to an orphanage, but Peg was so young, it was thought she would be better off in a home. Jack sort of disappeared after this tragedy and wasn't heard from for many years. Mom and Dad told Peg and Pat that they were like "sisters," and they raised Peg through high school. The two girls became close friends and played happily together most of the time.

According to my sister Pat, those years in Heartwell were wonderful. Dad built a tennis court on the property where friends often came over and had fun. He was a genius at making and fixing things. The Lynch home in Heartwell had a cistern (tank for holding rainwater) with a pump by the back door. Dad figured out how to bring water into a sink in the kitchen, which was still a rarity in the rural Midwest in the 1920s. The sink had one faucet. You turned on the water by pushing a button on an electric plate, which switched on a motor in the basement. The motor had a belt that went around a bicycle wheel and that machine pumped water into the sink. Brilliant! No one else had a rig like that to get water inside the house. The neighbors called it "Chester's invention."

My family may have had running water, but rural Nebraska hadn't yet provided sewers for its residents. Of course, Dad put his mind to improving their outhouse too. It was a long, low shed with three doors; the first door led to a small room that served as a coal shed. The middle door led to the outhouse toilet seats, which boasted both high and low "two-holed" seats. The third door was storage.

When Pat was in fourth grade (1933), Dad was informed that his services would no longer be required at the Heartwell School. This came as a shock to the family since he was well liked, had just led the high school basketball team through a winning season, and had even asked for a raise. The school board said that they couldn't afford him. My mother thought it might have more to do with the fact that some of the new school board members were known to be former Ku Klux Klan men, and were not fond of Catholics working for the district. Although initially I did not have much faith in Mom's theory, it may have some merit since other documentation shows that the Klan actually was very active in central Nebraska in the 1920s and '30s.

Whatever the reason, my family was in trouble without a job for my dad. Between 1933 and 1935, my dad could not find permanent work anywhere. He looked for teaching jobs outside of Heartwell with no luck. Those years were excruciating for all the plains states in the U.S. They were drought years, complete with dust storms and extreme heat—tough times for farmers and their communities. I remember my mother saying, "We wondered where did all the money go? Nobody in Heartwell had any money." Dad found whatever short jobs he could. He worked the section gang on the Burlington Railroad part time, worked on farms, helped on his folks' farm. He finally got on a Works Projects Administration (WPA) job that paid $45 a month, $50 when he was made foreman. Pat said she was embarrassed about our dad not having a steady job. The summer before she began the eighth grade, Dad finally found a permanent position on a well-drilling outfit on the Burlington Railroad. The catch was, he was gone all the time.

Finally, Mom decided she needed to stop waiting for my father to find a job and help move the family's fortunes along herself. As I mentioned before, she and her siblings (Jack, Mary, Anna, and Margaret) sued their brother, Mike O'Malley, for their share of their mother's estate. The case was settled and each O'Malley child got some money out of it. That settlement paid some bills, but Mom was determined to get out of Heartwell where she could get a job and Pat and Peg could attend a Catholic school. With Dad away on the job, the three females would get in the family's 1928 Chrysler and tour the towns in the area, looking for a better place to land. They drove through Minden, Kearney, Hastings, and Grand Island. Mom decided on Hastings because she liked St. Cecilia's, the church there. (Maybe she identified with the name!)

In 1936, entirely on her own, Mom bought a house at 812 W. 14th in Hastings with $2500 of the money from the lawsuit against her brother Mike, and the family moved. Dad's name never was on that house title. Pat and Peg started school there, and in October, Dad got laid off from the drilling crew and came to their new home. "Nice house!" he said. I think he approved of my mom's initiative. Mom could not find a job but she made friends. Peg and Pat got babysitting jobs to help with expenses. But Dad couldn't find work, which meant the family was really scraping to keep going.

At the same time, events on the Lynch family farm were getting dire. My grandfather, Philip, had gone blind. The dust storms had dried up the ground. Nothing could grow without water and topsoil, so people and animals alike were starving. Then, my uncle Ignatius died of tuberculosis in 1935 at age 37. This was my dad's younger brother. He never married and was the main labor source for the farm. Now he was gone, leaving an elderly woman and a blind man alone on 620 acres. It looked like the only thing to do was move from Hastings and try to help save the farm. So, in February or March of 1937, Dad loaded his clothes and tools into the Chrysler, and moved up to his parents' farm in Custer County, Nebraska. The farm was ten miles south of the town of Oconto, near a Lutheran Church and a deserted place called Buffalo, Nebraska. Lexington, Nebraska is about twenty miles south.

IV – Depression on the Lynch Farm

Back in Hastings, Pat and Peg were enjoying their school and friends. Saving a farm wasn't their idea of a great adventure. Pat had enrolled in a sewing class at the Y and made herself a halter top and some shorts. Neither wanted to move to the middle of nowhere, but the decision wasn't up to them.

Mom (Cecilia) started making preparations to vacate her house in Hastings. On their own, she and the girls moved all the family furniture to one of the upstairs bedrooms to allow the house to be rented in their absence. Pat remembered saying, "I think my mother is trying to kill us."

The following is an excerpt from Pat's letter to her granddaughter, Tara, about her memories of what happened next: "The day after school was out, we took the train from Hastings to Oconto. Grandpa (meaning Tara's grandpa, Pat's future husband, Dick DeBacker) and Eddy Laurence came to the depot to tell us goodbye. We only had two suitcases and two boxes, so we didn't bring much.

"Dad met us in the Chrysler and explained to us that Grandma (Catherine Lynch) had made an apartment for us in the big house. Well, when we drove the ten miles out, we went into a dining room door. She had made the dining room into a combination kitchen/dining room and the stairs to upstairs were in the dining room. We also had the four bedrooms upstairs. Grandma and Grandpa had the kitchen with sink, bathroom, bedroom, and parlor. All the doors to the dining room were shut and locked. So we were to use the outside toilet, get water from outside. The upstairs was a mess."

As Mom slowly absorbed the reality of their situation, an ominous quiet descended on the house. Then, she kind of lost her cool. "Where am I supposed to do dishes?! How are we supposed to get laundry done?! I have come to help and this is the thanks I get?!!" After that, Mom stormed upstairs and didn't come out of a back bedroom for nearly two days.

Again, from Pat's letter: "Meanwhile, Dad fixed a meal on the coal oil stove. He prided himself on the fact that he never raised his voice. But I rather sympathized with Mom." And who wouldn't? She had moved from a nice home that she paid for, in a town she loved, to a failing farm where she was locked out of the most useful rooms in the house. Talk about adding insult to injury!

Pat said that after a few days, Mom cooled off and adapted to life on the farm. She rearranged the upstairs furniture and figured out how to cope with the water situation, using the hose as a water supply. Peg and Pat got to know Grandpa Philip better and came to quite like him, calling him a "nice old man." Plus, Grandma made homemade donuts to go with tea. So, coming into their side of the house was a treat.

On their first day at the farm, Dad took Peg and Pat on a tour of the farm. Even though they were young teenagers, they could see that conditions were bad. Pat recalled, "The tractor didn't work. He had planted and cultivated with four old horses that were on their last legs. The chickens were a mess, the pigs had a disease, and the windmill wasn't pumping water. Practically all the peach trees were dead, also the grapevines. Grandpa always had beehives, but they had not been taken care of. We repeated all this to Mom and she said, 'Well we will just have to help Dad to get it organized and cleaned up. Peg, you work with me, and Pat, you work with your Dad.' Dad was delighted about all this."

Pat said that the family had a sense of optimism about working together and shaping things up. As they went to bed that night, it rained a little. That was the last rain they saw all summer. It seems their optimism was misplaced.

Pat's memories go on to describe hard labor, multigenerational differences, and moments of fun amid the hard times:

"Mom decided that she would cut down a dead peach tree every day and make a woodpile. She couldn't stand the dead trees and by September she had a pretty good-sized woodpile. She used a two-man saw – Peg or me on the other end."

"The dog died and so did one of the horses. Mom said there was a 'meaugh' on the place. Meaugh is Irish for a curse. After the dog was gone, the coyote would raid the chicken house. There were about 38 or 40 cows and one bull. Two of the cows were milk cows, so we had milk, cream, butter, and buttermilk, but not enough to sell. Only six or eight eggs a week."

"The thrashers came one day and cut the oats. Peg and I shucked oats and I learned I could work faster than my dad. Every day there was hot sun."

"I had only short shorts and a halter to wear and loved getting a great tan. This outfit bothered my Grandmother a lot and she would send me in the house or barn if anyone came and talked to me about modesty and purity. There wasn't a kid within ten miles all summer."

"Surprisingly, Peg and I had a lot of fun. We explored the canyons. Grandma had a basket with Indian arrowheads and rattlesnake rattles and we were always looking for Indian heads.We did go to Pressy Park a couple times to swim in the river on the Loup River between Oconto and Broken Bow."

"We brought in cows. I worked with Dad a lot, he let me drive all over in the Chrysler with the stick shift." As they worked together, he tried to explain why Grandma was like she was. "Be kind to her," Dad (Chester) urged. "Grandma is having a tough time with the idea of losing the farm. And Ignatius's death has been so sad." It probably wasn't easy for her to have a blind husband whose health was failing. And it must have been getting bad, because Philip didn't live much longer.

Pat told me Dad tried to keep spirits up. He would tell us, with a smile, "Wash the car, it will run better." As they got older, Pat and Peg would occasionally find one or two cigarettes apiece in their dresser drawers, unknown, of course, to my mother. Fortunately, they never did become real smokers. Dad didn't smoke cigarettes but apparently he did occasionally smoke a pipe.

By August of that summer, the pastures were dried out and the Sweeney family, our cousins, came up from Grand Island to buy the cows, excepting two milk cows and the bulls. They also bought furniture, dishes and whatever else they could find that was useful. Around the same time, Philip and Catherine said they were going to retire in Grand Island and go to the doctors there. They left in August '37 and the family never did see them again. Pat recalled the sense of relief after they departed. "It was better with them gone and we could use the kitchen." Philip died in 1938, not long after they left for Grand Island. His obituary described Philip W. Lynch as, "A kind and loving father, beloved by all who knew him." Catherine passed away eight years later in 1946. She was my last grandparent. I was four years old. I think I recall her in her coffin. Mom said they had a visitation or viewing at the "big house." It rained hard and the hearse got stuck crossing the creek, which caused the actual funeral to be delayed.

Before she left, Grandma indicated that Pat probably couldn't go to high school as there wasn't any money for it, but school was very important to my mother. Cecilia went to the bank and borrowed money for high school. She made arrangements for 14-year-old Pat to stay with the McDermott family in Oconto for $2.50 a week so she could attend ninth grade. Peg, who was 13 at the time, walked three miles to the country school to attend to her studies in the lower grade. Since Pat only had the shorts and halter top to wear, Cecilia made two dresses for her—by hand, because (as with everything on the farm) the sewing machine was broken. Pat said in her letter that she just washed out underwear and socks herself at the McDermotts' but had fun staying in town. Every evening the kids gathered up on Main Street until dark, and she made friends quickly.

Back on the farm, conditions were not getting any better. The family was still under water with the bank. Crops weren't producing. Then, just before Christmas of 1938, Dad had a recurrence of an illness they thought was pleurisy and wasn't feeling well. Mom wrote her brother Jack (Peg's father), who now lived in Paxton, Nebraska and asked if he could come get the girls. He arrived the day after Christmas. So, Pat and Peg loaded up their belongings and went to Paxton to live with Peg's father, his new wife, Mary Riordan O'Malley, and Peg's two brothers, who were back from the orphanage. Pat says the first thing their new guardians did was to buy them some better clothes. She said there was more food at Jack's house than she had seen in a long time. In particular, she remembered a pink angel food cake that was made for her birthday that year. It must have been some hungry times on the farm.

Though Dad and Mom tried their hardest to save the Lynch family farm, the efforts failed. The Oconto bank foreclosed on the land and the big house somewhere between 1939 and 1941.

Losing the farm was probably the best thing for Dad at the time, though I know it was hard on him too. However, his health was quite worrisome to everyone. It was bad enough that he couldn't even drive any more. I don't know how, but Mom gathered up her gumption and drove Dad to Hastings to see the doctor. She didn't drive much back then, but she must have figured it out. Then, back at the house in Hastings, she moved all the furniture out of the upstairs bedroom back to where it belonged.

Dad's "pleurisy" (kind of a generic term at that time for chest pain) turned out to be heart problems, and he was to take it easy. He had gotten hired back as Superintendent in Heartwell for the coming fall. The day after school got out for spring semester, Jack drove Pat and Peg back to Hastings to rejoin Mom and Dad there. So all was well again, more or less. The girls had moved four times in less than two years. Pat said later, the experience formed a solid base for her future ability to cope. "It gave us a lot of good experience when nothing seemed to go right," she said. The next March, Mom had twins who died at birth, so life—and death—continued.

I don't understand everything about Dad being let go by the Heartwell School Board in 1933 and being rehired a few years later. I have tried to research this but no appropriate reason is apparent to me. Probably some prejudice was involved, as Mom certainly felt. A couple of school board changes at that time appear very unusual. However, it was a tough time for everyone, I suppose, and maybe school board finances were part of the problem. What I do know is that my mother thought it was very unfair, which is why she refused to live in Heartwell when Dad was rehired.

Fortunately, she always had wonderful memories of the students that she and Dad had known and taught. In 1974, Mom was delighted to be invited to the Heartwell High School alumni reunion. Former Heartwell High School teachers were being honored, especially my father and Miss Henigan, who were both long-time teachers. Both were let go in 1933 by the school board and rehired later. My sister Pat, Mom and I attended the reunion. My mother was very excited to attend.

It was a beautiful June day. The former students, all adult men and women of course, were gathered on the school lawn when we pulled up. They milled around her as she walked slowly across the grounds. She was delighted to see them and they appeared just as pleased to see her. Despite her previous stroke, she recognized and warmly greeted many of the former students. They also warmly welcomed Pat, who had attended grade school in Heartwell, but they were completely bewildered by me, especially when I claimed to be Pat's brother. As one former student said, "You can't be Mrs. Lynch's son. I saw them at mass on Sundays and there were only two little girls, no boys." I tried to explain that I was born later, in 1942 when Mom was 46 and Dad was 50 years old. Finally, I let it be and just enjoyed Mom's delight in visiting with everyone. It was a wonderful day that had been much too long in coming.

Mom died four months later, October 1974, in Grand Island, Nebraska.

In a quirky twist of fate, our family's connection to the "big house" my grandfather built outside of Oconto wasn't quite done yet. About 1970, give or take a few years, it was decided to move the house from its original location on the Lynch homestead to Lexington, Nebraska, about twenty miles away. I have no idea who actually owned the big house when it was being moved to Lexington. My best guess is that maybe the Lynches were trying to salvage it though they had lost the farmland many years before.

The person who was hired to move the house was Leo Brennan, my cousin on the O'Malley side. (His mother, Anna, was one of my mother's older sisters.) Unfortunately, while rounding a turn in the road, the house slipped off the truck, went off the pavement, and careened down into a valley, breaking into many pieces as it bounced down the hill. I can just imagine the workers standing at the top of the hill, surveying the many shards of what had once been a home. Hands on hips, mouths open in shock and horror, they must have felt absolutely awful for the loss—not just because it was a professional embarrassment, but THAT house in particular was the worst possible home for an O'Malley relative to be losing control over.

Years later, I talked with Leo's oldest son about it at a family reunion. He wasn't in charge of the business then, but even after decades had passed, he didn't find the incident funny at all. Neither did his dad when he was alive. I recall Leo as a fun, extroverted guy who loved to laugh, but he never joked about that accident. Personally, I couldn't help but smile at the idea of one of my O'Malley-side relatives (Leo Brennan) destroying the original Lynch-side homestead house. Probably not good for family dynamics.

CHAPTER 2

My Early Years

I – Dad's Final Years

The family breathed a sigh of relief when my father (Chester Lynch) got his job back with the school district in Heartwell. It seems the feeling was mutual. The town had really missed him and citizens weren't happy with the new direction the school board was taking things. So, the new school board traveled up to the farm to ask Dad if he would come back.

That was fortuitous timing. Dad's health was not up to farm work, and all that backbreaking labor wasn't making much of a difference anyway. Working with young people was what Dad really liked to do. He was much more than just a teacher. Hired as the Superintendent in Heartwell, Dad was very busy with enrollment, teaching, and activities. He was the baseball and basketball coach and taught science, mathematics, and Latin, as well as occasional voluntary classes for interested students in the evening. At the time, Heartwell still had a population of about 200.

Recently, I had the special opportunity to visit with one of my father's former students, Mrs. Lona Kuehn, at the Baptist Home in Minden, Nebraska. Now 100 years old, Mrs. Kuehn graduated from Heartwell High School in the 1930s. When I introduced myself, she gave me a big smile and said how kind I was to visit her. When I asked about my father, she said, "He was stern but not, uh…uh…

obnoxious." We both laughed. She said, "I really liked him. He taught mathematics, and I was good at math. We all did math problems on the blackboard. When I got done, I would turn around and look at him. He would smile and say, 'Just wait, Lona, until the others are done.'"

After visiting for a while, I moved to leave. Mrs. Kuehn called me back, grabbed my hands, and said, "Your father was a great man." I was pleased, of course, and I do think she liked my father, but I also thought it was very kind of her to say that—to make sure that she told me what I wanted to hear. What a fine lady.

I loved Mrs. Kuehn's phrase, "He was stern but not obnoxious." That must have been true. Mom said she was always jealous about how he would just come to the classroom door at the beginning of class, and all went quiet. She said, "My students never did that for me. I always had to yell at them to be quiet."

With all the time and effort my father devoted to his students, it might have made sense for my family to move back to Heartwell instead of living in Hastings. That way he wouldn't have to go back and forth. There are only twenty miles between the two towns, but remember this was the 1930s. Cars, roads, and attitudes about commutes were different than they are now. In a planning discussion Dad said, "There's nothing in the world I'd love to do more than go back to Heartwell." My mother said, "I will never live in that town again for letting you go." That was pretty much the end of the discussion.

My mom, Pat, and Peg lived in her house in Hastings. My dad rented a room from the Filkin family in Heartwell to stay in during the week. Years later, John Filkin was a pallbearer at Dad's funeral. Living alone in Heartwell made him even more devoted to his students, because they were all he had to hold his attention on weeknights. On weekends, he took a bus back to the family home in Heartwell.

That's how it went for four years. Back and forth, back and forth. The farm was foreclosed on. My grandfather passed away. And still Dad went back and forth from his job in Heartwell to the family in Hastings. During one of those weekend visits, I was conceived. I was born in Hastings on March 22, 1942. Mom and Dad named me Joseph Daniel Lynch. They had planned to name me Daniel, but Mom told me that since I was born so close to St. Joseph's feast day (March 19th), they decided to name me Joseph. Close enough, I guess. Pat was 18 years old when I was born, and Peg was 17. Pat was attending the College of Saint Mary (CSM) in Omaha. When she came home and saw Mom in maternity clothes, she told Mom it was "not funny at all!" (Little did she know.) Pat had a scholarship for tuition at CSM but there wasn't enough money to keep paying room and board. Between the lack of money, my birth, and the onset of World War II, Pat dropped out of college, took my mother's advice, moved to California, and got a job as part of the war effort.

My earliest memories do include my father, but they are vague. In those foggy recollections, he was a sick man, often too tired to do anything but rest on the couch or in bed.

I don't recall Mom mentioning it to me but Dad's obituary states that from 1942-46 he worked at the US Naval Ammunition Depot in Hastings. It also noted his work during the Depression (1930s) for the Work Projects Administration. (The WPA was President Roosevelt's massive effort to hire the unemployed.) Once, when I asked Mom if he really worked for the WPA, she answered rather proudly (or maybe defensively), "Yes, and they made him a *foreman*."

At some point, Dad's heart condition forced him to stop teaching. When he was unable to work regularly, Mom wanted him to take care of me at home, but he really wasn't up to it most of the time. I remember reading with him, playing catch, and sort of hanging out. There wasn't a lot he could physically do to entertain a little kid. Our family wouldn't have a TV for many years. Games like tag and hide and seek probably weren't on the agenda, but his presence infuses my memories of early life with a sense of kindness. I remember him reading to me, and eventually teaching me to read at a pretty tender age, probably about four years old.

I'm guessing that for Dad, the time we spent reading must have been bittersweet. Knowing his time on Earth was short can't have been easy. He would be leaving a wife alone to raise a young child by herself, and Cecilia had limited formal education and not much work history to lean on other than her previous teaching in a one-room school near Grand Island. She really didn't drive, and she was the world's worst cook. But perhaps knowing that there wouldn't be a lifetime of memories ahead allowed Dad to soak in the joy of being with a young child rather than worrying about mowing the lawn or paying the bills. I hope so.

For my part, it's tragic to lose a parent when you are that young because you can't remember much about them. Most of my memories of Dad are borrowed from the stories other people have told me, although every so often pieces of him that were dormant inside me reveal themselves, like a ray of light through a cloud. For instance, one day when I was an adult, I was tying my shoes and an observer noticed my method was unusual. She asked, "Why do you tie your shoes that way?" I said, "What are you talking about?" She said, "You tie your shoes all strange. It takes twice as long and it's awkward." Have you ever stopped in the middle of putting your shoes on and wondered why or how you came to use that method? Of course not. Your hands just follow the pattern so you can finish the task and get going. I didn't know the answer to her question; I just knew that's how I had always done it.

And then a year later or so, I found myself in a repeat of the conversation. Only this time, the person said, "Why do you use a left-handed tie? You're right-handed." "Huh?" "People who are left-handed can tie their shoes that way." And I thought, oh...my dad was left-handed. How's that for a moment? I have no recollection of him teaching me to tie or do any of those small self-care tasks, but every now and then the lessons he taught me come through.

Probably my earliest vivid memory is the time I broke my leg while wandering alone in the Hastings cemetery. I was five years old. I wasn't supposed to be out of the yard, but as kids do, I wandered a bit and discovered that I could climb up on the headstones. Sadly, the one I picked wasn't planted well, and I pulled the whole thing over on myself and broke my leg. I can't remember how I was discovered or how long I lay there with the pain in my leg.

I don't know a lot of detail about my father's last years, but I can imagine that the realization of Dad's imminent death had to weigh heavily on both my parents' minds. My dad's health was failing, but he still needed care. I was about four or five. Pat had moved away by then, so there were two people for my mom to care for without help—and she needed to finish her education degree in a hurry. You can imagine how terribly worried and guilty Dad must have felt. After some time, Dad literally didn't seem to be dying, so he thought, "I'll try and get a job." He was hired to teach in Okaton, South Dakota for the 1947-48 school year. So, we moved again. The school there was quite large, but located in a town of only 200 people. I guess it got its higher enrollment numbers by drawing in all the rural farm kids from the surrounding area. My father taught fifth grade in that two-story school. Incidentally, while writing this book in 2016, I visited that school building and discovered that it still stands and is being converted to a single-family home by a young couple who live there (the old schoolhouse in Heartwell is also apparently being converted to a single family home).

Probably because my parents tried to shield me from the bulk of the fear, I didn't understand how bad things were for our family until I saw the reactions of other people who interacted with us. When I was five, I got my tonsils out at the Kadoka hospital (about thirty miles from Okaton). Even though that was a lifetime ago, I still remember that it hurt like a bitch, especially when they gave me toast to eat afterwards! I also remember being quite impressed with the dumbwaiter that brought my toast and other meals up from a lower floor. A young doctor at the hospital was especially kind, and I remember thinking, *He's really being nice to me for some reason.* Probably, he knew about my dad's condition and felt sorry for me.

Not long after that, my dad was hospitalized for his heart disease at the same hospital in Kadoka. It's funny, but my biggest recollection from visiting Dad in the hospital was his urinal. You know how five-year-olds are about bodily functions.

After suffering from his heart condition for ten years, Patrick Francis Chester Lynch died of heart failure on March 25, 1948, at age 56, three days after my sixth birthday. He was well loved by his family and by most people who knew him. He was an inventor, an educator, a father and husband, a loyal son. Those who came into contact with him in his prime were amazed by his willingness to try and solve problems, whether it was fixing tractors, getting water from the well to the kitchen, or building a tennis court in Heartwell so the community could have a place to recreate.

When my father died he received nothing from the state of Nebraska for his years of teaching school. Mom received a small amount of money for the time Dad worked for the Burlington Northern Railroad in the summers and also a small amount of Social Security until I was 18 years old. His only real asset in the world was a $1,000 Knights of Columbus life insurance policy, which probably covered burial costs.

It still makes me sad to think of how much that life force was diminished in Dad's last years. Probably, those who met him then thought little of him. That impression was proven true the time in the 1990s, I stopped in Okaton and got gas at the Texaco station. While filling up, I met an "old timer" in overalls sitting in a chair. He asked, "What brings you here?" I replied, "My parents taught here in 1947-48, and my father actually died while he was teaching school here." He said, "Nope, didn't happen. I lived here all my life, and no teacher ever died like that here." I think my father was a good man and made an impression on a reasonable number of people, but apparently not in Okaton.

While grieving, Mom actually finished out the term teaching in Dad's position. At age six, I came to school with her and sat at the back of the fifth-grade room since there was nowhere else for me to go. I don't know how she managed the strength to get up every day and teach when she must have been so sad and scared. But she did.

II – Mom & Me, Finding Our Footing Alone

Mom was in a tough spot. My dad had really taken care of everything for our family. He cooked most of the meals when he was home. He drove the car. He worked and supported us financially. My parents thought themselves quite educated considering the time they lived in. In fact, once, when they had a little extra money, their idea of a wonderful luxury was to subscribe to the *Atlantic Monthly* magazine for one year. Mom was terribly proud of the knowledge she and my father had earned, but perhaps to her detriment, she knew more about literature than everyday living.

It seemed that some of my mother's siblings had opinions about her likelihood of succeeding on her own. They thought of her as bookish and unable to do anything useful. Her older sister Mary said to my mom, "You are not going to be able to raise Joe. Someone will end up taking him away from you, and we will have to raise him."

I think my mom was determined to prove her siblings wrong. It was true that she lacked real-world skills when my father died, but they didn't realize how strong-willed Cecilia O'Malley Lynch actually was. As evidenced by that house she bought and moved into and out of in Hastings, Nebraska, my mom *could* fend for herself when she had to. Starting in 1948, Mom no longer had a choice. She would have to provide a life for herself and for me full time. Before Dad grew sick and died, Mom didn't often step outside her comfort zone. But his death changed her. It forced her to find a way into the world. Mom overcame her own fears and the perceptions of her family, though they weren't often far from her mind. She actually said a few times, "If you get in trouble, they are going to take you away because they don't think I can raise you." She didn't push that, but it got mentioned from time to time.

To try to find a way to support the family, two months after my father's death my mom enrolled in summer school at Black Hills State Teachers College in Spearfish, South Dakota. She already possessed a two-year teaching certificate from 1921, back when she was very young, but she was aiming for a four-year degree. Mom's 1921 certification from Nebraska State Teachers College at Kearney said she was qualified to teach anywhere in the state of Nebraska; actually the wording on the certificate is the darnedest thing. It says she is: "Approved to teach in the State of Nebraska forever without further education." I said to her once, "Why didn't you stay in Nebraska?" She said "out west" was where the jobs were and Nebraska paid nothing. Also, I bet she wanted to put some space between the two of us and the rest of the family who harbored so many doubts about her fitness to raise me. So, she was determined to get her education and teach in other, perhaps higher-paying, states.

Summer school didn't go well. Mom's grades were absolutely abysmal. I recently pulled out my old papers and found her report cards from back then. They showed Ds and Fs, mostly. She must have been terribly stressed.

That time period was a crossroads for my mom. Years after the fact, she told me she just made a conscious decision to move forward. Sitting in the house where Dad used to live, surrounded by pictures of him, books they had purchased together, and the record player he used to listen to...it was just too hard to cope. So, Mom made a plan. She took all his photos off the wall and put them away except for one by her bed. She put the record player away and replaced it with a radio. "This is the music of right now. And that was the music of a time passed," she told herself. One regret she carried about that transformation was about Dad's books. She explained as an elderly woman, "We had to move forward. So I made all those changes. I threw away all Dad's books except the Shakespeare, Sir Walter Scott, and Robert Browning. That's the worst thing I ever did. I should have never thrown away so many of his books."

The September after my father's death, Mom's only job offer was in St. Maries, Idaho. So, that's where we went. I went to a Catholic school there. My teacher was a nun who I think was a very good lady, but I remember not liking her at all. I had a tendency of playing with myself (as small boys often do), and she didn't buy that at all. She never hit anyone, but she was very strict. It was a "Yes, Sister. Thank you, Sister" kind of classroom, with no room for anything else.

It was also tricky to place me academically because I could read very well (thanks to my father's efforts), but I didn't know how to write or do any math. Kindergarten didn't really exist in rural Nebraska and South Dakota, and I hadn't gone to first grade. I couldn't form written letters and I was quite immature, due to being younger than the other kids and having had little previous classroom experience. They eventually settled on starting me in the second grade because of my reading ability.

I still kind of stuck out as a problem kid, unaccustomed to the rigors of serious classroom responsibilities. Crayons were a problem too. You see, I'm partially color-blind, but I didn't know it at the time. I didn't discover my color-blindness until I was in college. At age six, I just thought I was bad at coloring because I had never been to a real school previously. In order to properly fill in green trees and red Santa suits, I needed the "good crayons," the newer ones with labels so I could read the names of the colors. And if some other kid had the audacity to suggest that they should have a turn with those colors, I would object.

We were only in St. Maries one year. A couple of years later we visited St. Maries and I discovered that the "strict" nun—the most intimidating teacher ever—was a close friend of and absolutely in cahoots with my mother. They hugged and cried like the greatest of friends upon their reunion, and that's when I realized that when she was so strict, she was just doing what she and my mother thought was best for me.

At the end of our year in St. Maries, my mom still didn't have her four-year teaching degree, so she was forced to take the leftover jobs that other teachers didn't want. At the end of summer each year, she would apply to small-town schools that didn't have a qualified instructor yet and were starting to get desperate to fill the slot before school started. Then, at the last moment, she would take whatever job became available.

That method of job-searching is how we found ourselves in Paisley, Oregon the following September. Paisley is in southern Oregon, but nothing else is. Really there's nothing there. Oregon is known for coastlines and lush redwood forests. Then there's a pocket of flat land in south-central Oregon that includes Paisley. A visit to the town of 200 will reveal sagebrush, rock, and (dry) alkali lakes. The most remarkable thing I can recall from our time in Paisley was the flooding of the Chewaucan River. That was a pretty big deal; imagine knee-high water flooding right down the center of the main street.

I remember a couple of teachers in Paisley, including the Mahoneys, who were Catholic, young, had small kids, and used to go to mass with us. They moved on after one year. Then there was Mrs. Bennett, my teacher for both years we were there. She was a good friend of my mother's but she certainly believed in physical punishment for misbehaving in class. It didn't hurt that much and most of the time I deserved it. Some days I would come home from her music class, happily singing *Onward Christian Soldiers* and other similar songs, and my mother would mutter that she wished that Mrs. Bennett would teach me something other than her Methodist Church songs. I learned a lot in Paisley, including everything about the birds and bees from a classmate. I didn't believe him, but he had it all correct.

One other memory that stands out from Paisley is my first-ever experience with a bully. Being the perpetual new kid, I often got singled out by the hooligans who had something to prove. In Paisley, one kid just wouldn't quit. He was always saying he was going to fight me after school. I never knew why. I hadn't done anything to him that I could remember. His threats scared me though. He was much bigger and could easily have made good on his constant threats to "kill me." So one day, I finally fought him on the playground after school. I hit him with a perfect punch, right in the nose. Blood went everywhere! Funny how you always remember the perfect punch. Except it still didn't do any good. Even as the guy stopped punching, he was saying, "I'm gonna get you for that. I'm gonna beat you to a…" He continued that sort of talk the whole time I lived there. He never again tried to fight me, but I wasn't certain that he wouldn't. Despite my glorious stand, the whole experience was confusing and scary for me.

If you go about twenty-five miles south of Paisley, you hit the next town, Valley Falls, population two, just a gas station and an RV park. Another twenty-five miles down the road was Lakeview, Oregon, which is where we drove to CCD on Saturday and mass on Sunday morning (CCD is religious education for Catholic public school kids). I remember getting along well with the nuns teaching CCD. I think that my kick-start in education from the "Meanest Sister Ever" probably set me up for success. I discovered that the nuns just wanted you to be quiet in class and memorize the prayers. That was easy for me, and it was all they really asked of us. For example, they would give us homework each week to learn a prayer like the Hail Mary. So if you showed up the next week and you knew the Hail Mary, they were happy.

There weren't very many Catholics in Paisley, but there was one prominent family, the O'Learys, who owned a large cattle ranch. One year they invited Mom and me to the ranch for Christmas. Mom was very pleased. So was I, but for a different reason. I thought Mary O'Leary, a girl in my class, was the prettiest girl in the entire school. However, I don't recall her ever noticing me. The O'Learys were always very kind to my mother.

There was a small Catholic church in Paisley, and one Sunday a month an old priest came from Lakeview and said Mass. There weren't many people there, and in the winter we would all gather in the sacristy around the wood stove to keep warm while the priest put on his vestments for mass. One week we had a mission, and had to go to church every evening, which I thought was a bit much. Mostly, I remember the church freezing and the priest being very old and frail. He always sat in a chair when he gave his sermons or made announcements. Despite all the church stuff in Paisley, in Lakeview, and at home, I still had to go to church summer school in Omaha or Grand Island because I was a public school kid.

We stayed in Paisley for two years when I was in third and fourth grades. I remember coming home from school each day to our tiny rental house. In winter, the house was freezing. While it *was* the 1950s, we hadn't reached the standard of living that included central heat or even radiators. There was just a wood stove in the center of the house. As you can guess, money was very tight for Mom. She wasn't a fully certified teacher, so she took what she could get from the meager offerings proffered by those rural school districts. The routine that we grew into together was: get home, start a fire, go take a nap for an hour. Teaching all day was exhausting for my mom, and I was always glad for a bit of quiet time to rest or read or whatever. Then when naptime was done, the house would be warm and she'd get up and fix dinner.

Well...we called it dinner. Mom was the worse cook I ever knew. When I went to college, I was amazed and delighted by the variety and quality of the cafeteria food. Mom cooked everything on high, as if to be done with it as quickly as possible. All the fried eggs had black rims. If we ever had meat, you knew it was done when it reached the consistency of a hockey puck.

During those first two summers when it was just me and Mom, she attended summer school in Cheney, Washington (Eastern Washington College of Education) and in Spearfish, South Dakota (Black Hills State Teachers College). She tried to keep me with her, but it really wasn't possible to keep an eye on me and attend class and study. So starting the summer of 1950 or '51, Mom farmed me out to my sister Pat, who lived in Omaha, Nebraska at that time.

The first couple of years, Mom and I made the journey from Pendleton, Oregon to Nebraska on the Union Pacific train. I loved traveling by train! They had black porters who would give you a crisp, white pillow for a quarter. Most of our meals were sandwiches and things we brought on ourselves, but we got one meal in the dining car. I remember enjoying watching the countryside flow by while being served a hot meal by waiters. We didn't get to restaurants any other times, so it was a special occasion for me.

One time the train stopped in Pocatello, Idaho. Mom and I got off to stretch our legs and the train pulled out without us, which was bad enough, but it became worse when I told Mom I didn't have my shoes on. I'd left them on the train. I did get new shoes, but Mom was not pleased.

After two years of train travel, Mom opted to drive to Nebraska instead. She probably needed the car with her since she was attending summer classes in Kearney, Nebraska while I stayed with Pat, who had moved to Grand Island. In general, we would drive back and forth on Highway 30. Highway 30 is the road that today's Interstate 80 replaced.

Mom never did become a comfortable driver. Every time we would begin a journey, she would start driving while we said the rosary together in the car. Joining the highway from Paisley caused her a great deal of anxiety. Mom would creep down the highway at maybe 40 mph while gripping the wheel as if it might fly off. By the end of the trip we were a little better—maybe even pretty good drivers. I say we because she made it clear after a while that I wasn't just along for the ride. Even though I was only 8 or 9, I shared the responsibility to make sure we got to our destination in one piece.

One year, I was on map duty and fell asleep. She woke me up, pretty mad. She said, "You can't sleep. Who's gonna do the map?" And I realized that "Navigator" wasn't an honorary title. I thought I was just doing it for the fun of it, but that wasn't the case. One year, we got into Boise, Idaho and the road markings had changed. It was the first year the stoplights had arrows telling you when it was okay to turn left or go ahead, etc. She had no idea, literally no idea what to do at all. I had to say, "I think we can go left," when the arrow was pointing left. It was a little scary, but Mom still made it to Pat's. God bless her.

The year I was 12, my duties increased again. Mom was driving down the highway in Wyoming, nothing but sagebrush and clouds as far as you can see, and Mom stopped the 1949 Chevrolet right in the middle of the highway. She put it in park and said, "It's time for you to learn to drive."

I said, "What?!"

She replied, "What if I got sick? You'd have to drive." So, I slid over and gave it my best. We didn't wreck.

Mom and I didn't play together in the way you see parents do now. But she did love to swim and soak in hot springs. There was a hot springs pool near Paisley that we went to occasionally. I was never too sure about the hot temperature of the water and the pungent sulfur smell, but Mom enjoyed it. We would also stop most years at Lava Hot Springs in Idaho when we were driving back and forth to Nebraska. Those were the few times I remember her goofing off a bit. Much of the rest of the time, she was a stern woman. She was kind and loving, especially to me, and she did laugh, certainly, but she wasn't always a lot of fun. I think life for her was probably pretty serious business. Those moments, especially at Lava Hot Springs, were some of the few times that I remember her relaxing and really enjoying herself.

Riding back and forth with Mom from Oregon or Washington to Nebraska was fun. It usually took three or four days. We would count the miles we traveled each day. Sometimes we spent a night in Nampa, Idaho with her brother, Jack O'Malley, his wife Mary and their son, my cousin Bob who was a few years older than me. One summer I spent a couple of weeks there. I really looked up to Bob and enjoyed being with him. I remember he tried to play a prank on me by putting salt in the sugar bowl, and encouraged me to put more and more so-called "sugar" on my cereal when I complained it tasted funny. Unfortunately for him, his mother baked a cake using the doctored sugar, which was really salt, and she served it to a ladies' group. He really, really got in trouble. Bob and his wife Mary live in Murphy, Idaho now.

Mom and her brother, Jack, stayed very close over the years. In later years, Jack would come up from his home in Nampa to Toppenish and spend a week or so fixing things around her house, painting the house, building steps, and so on.

III – Summers with Pat & the DeBackers

Those summer months with Pat and her family were an important part of my life. The first two or three summers were in Omaha with Pat and her family. The rest of the summers, until I was into high school, were spent at the home they bought in Grand Island, Nebraska, just twenty-five miles north of her childhood home in Hastings. My sister Patricia was called Patsy by most everybody, even some of her kids, especially when she got older, but I always called her Pat. Since she was 18 years older than me, our relationship resembled one of a mother and son. As we grew older, it evolved into a very special brother-sister bond. She is no longer alive, but when we were adults she sort of functioned as an advisor, family historian, and fellow comrade-in-arms, all rolled into one very special big sister.

During the summers, I lived with Pat and her husband, Dick DeBacker. I was six years older than their oldest child (Susan). As the years went by, I felt much more like a brother, not an uncle, to their eleven kids. I jumped right into the rhythm of the family with the DeBacker children after I arrived. We all had chores assigned each morning. We all rotated doing dishes, and there were lots of dishes! We mowed the lawn, cleaned the basement, cleaned the garage, etc. I remember Pat lecturing about the true meaning of doing dishes. "Doing dishes doesn't just mean do the dishes. It also means, clear the table, wipe it, sweep the floor, and straighten up the kitchen and dining room." Each morning, Pat would set out the food and make the plan for the day. The older kids, especially the girls, got a job like make lunch, or start dinner. And there was no arguing about it. When I got my assignment, I would go to tidy and sweep in the garage, or mow the lawn or whatever, until noon. For me, afternoons were usually free time to do whatever I wanted.

With a family that large, there had to be structure to make sure everyone got fed and the house stayed clean, especially since both Pat and her husband worked. Money was tight, so Pat worked with developmentally disabled adults. That willingness to accept and help those with developmental delays and genetic conditions set a good example for me, one that would be useful much later in my life.

Pat's husband, Dick, was a lawyer in private practice. Then he was appointed a judge but he didn't really like that job, even though it meant a regular paycheck and a good retirement plan. I remember him saying the child cases were the toughest.

I said, "Oh, because the parents are fighting with each other, and you have to decide which one would be better for the child?"

He said, "No, in most of these cases, neither parent should be allowed access to that child. And I am supposed to choose one."

I had real sympathy for him and understood why he quit. Besides, his ulcer was bleeding over the stress.

Dinnertime at Pat and Dick's also had a routine to it. Pat rotated a regular menu about every two weeks. After playing all afternoon, I looked forward to coming home and opening the door to the smell of dinner cooking—except on liver night. Then I would open the door and think, *Oh God. Liver.* I detested liver night, but it was probably a cheap cut of meat and there were a lot of mouths to feed. None of us kids got to pick and choose what was on our plates, but my brother-in-law Dick found a work-around. He liked to sit at the head of the big table and serve the plates. Each plate got a scoop of everything and would get passed down. He was the last one to be served and I'm pretty sure he made certain there were no remaining portions of whatever he didn't want. Years later, the DeBacker kids and I would talk about the mysterious way Dick (their dad) never had any peas on his plate.

In some ways, Dick served as a substitute father to me. I only saw him in the summers, but I think he tried to help teach me the things that a dad would. Dick took me to baseball games. I especially loved the old Omaha Cardinals in the Western League. Later, he occasionally took me to things like his Saturday morning coffees with his lawyer friends.

He was elected Hall County Attorney. It is very unusual for a Democrat to get elected for anything in rural Nebraska. Unfortunately, when he ran for re-election the campaign against him was very unfair and came down to counting the absentee ballots, which was done the day after the actual election. He took me with him to observe the counting of the absentee ballots. It was interesting, but unfortunately he lost.

When I was in college he took me hunting a couple of times, but I didn't enjoy it much. It was cold and my color-blindness didn't help. I asked him if he enjoyed hunting and he said he could take it or leave it. So I asked him why we were doing this.

There was a pause, and then Dick said, "Because you asked me to. At your dad's funeral when you were six, you looked up at me and said, 'Who's gonna teach me how to hunt?' I thought you wanted to learn this. I thought you needed to learn this."

I appreciated Dick's desire to fulfill that promise, but I never did grow to like hunting. I went duck hunting a couple of times in Toppenish but all I remember is how cold it was. My dad left me his rifle, but I just wasn't any good at it.

During the summers, Pat and Dick also took me camping in the Snowy Range in Wyoming with their family. After a few summers, they asked me if it was okay for "Gerry" to go in place of me, since she had never gone and had been living with them for a number of years. I thought how dumb and inconsiderate it was of me not to have thought of it myself. Of course, she should go instead of me.

Gerry (Gerarda Perez) was a couple of years older than me, and was sort of like a foster child who came to them from Catholic Charities or some similar organization because her parents were gone or unavailable or something. Her younger brother was living in Boys' Town in Omaha. She went to school, helped with the kids and around the house, and was always nice to me. I liked her. She eventually went to college for a while but had some sort of troubles. I have no idea where she is now.

Summers in Omaha were hot and sweaty, especially at night. This being long before anyone had air conditioning, I would lie in bed at 3613 Marcy Street with the windows open, trying to decide if it was cooler with a sheet or without one. I also remember the overwhelming stench from the stockyards in south Omaha drifting in on the breeze. People said those were the largest stockyards in the U.S. That's a lot of cows...and a lot of manure.

Mom didn't usually visit much during those months, though I do remember her sending me quite a few letters. She always told me she loved me and to be good for Pat.

During those summer months in Kearney, Mom chipped away at her four-year degree. Up until then, she had just been enrolling at whatever teachers' college was close by. One summer when she enrolled at Kearney, someone finally put a stop to this madness. Mom later told me that a professor sat her down one day and said, "Cecilia, you're never going to get a degree. Not the way you're doing it. You have been to the University of Nebraska, Omaha University, Kearney, and you have credits from all kinds of other schools. You're going here, you're going there." He said, "You have to come back here every summer. I'll be your advisor. And you'll get a degree, but you have to do what I say." She agreed with a sigh of relief. Then as they reviewed her transcripts, she started pointing out all the classes she had taken that didn't quite match the program's criteria.

"Well, my transcript says that I was in this class in 1919. I actually never took that class, so you better mark it out. I took a different class that is not listed here."

And he said, "No! If you tell them that, they'll take that out, but they won't replace it with the one you did take. We're lucky you've managed to get some granddaddy clause that still counts your credits, but you can't be changing the transcripts. If you say you didn't take something, you lose that credit, and there's no way they'll put History in there instead of Latin."

I don't know who that man was. God bless him. Mom got her degree from Nebraska State Teachers College at Kearney with the help of that kind man, though it took her several more summers. She finally earned her bachelor's degree in 1957 at the age of 61. Mom had completed that previous two-year teacher's program in 1921. It took her another 36 years to finish her four-year degree. Clearly, it was important to her. When she finally graduated, Mom said to me, "One day you will realize what this means, to get a degree at this age. You don't understand today, but you will."

Recently, I reviewed her final transcript from Kearney. She had credits from eight different universities between 1917 and 1957.

IV – Bay Center

In 1953, Mom and I lived in Bay Center, Washington. I spent my fifth- and sixth-grade years in that tiny harbor town on Washington's coast. Bay Center is situated on cliffs that look out over Willapa Bay. Barely hanging off the edge of the continent, the town is .4 square miles, with a population that varies between 175 and 300 people who mostly log and fish for a living. It has a post office and a three-room grade school (now closed) where my mom was one of three teachers. Though tiny, the town is where I started to see myself as an individual, where I began stating strong preferences about what I did and did not like to do. And it's where Mom continued stretching her limits of comfort.

Bay Center is kind of sheltered by the Long Beach Peninsula to its west. Willapa Bay is actually an estuary with tides that come and go. Sometimes when the tide was out, it was dry and you could look out over the bay and see a bear walking across from the peninsula. I remember being repeatedly warned about the danger of the caves in the side of the cliffs. With the tide out, there were all kinds of wonders to explore. When it came back in, the land—and the ability to leave the bay—swiftly disappeared. Neglect the incoming tide, and a person could be trapped in the caves that filled to the top with seawater.

I remember exploring those caves a little, but not too much. I was a cautious person then. I'm still that way. I carried a little book with the tide schedules to be sure I wouldn't be caught out in the bay at the wrong moment. I can remember climbing down the cliff's edge, just hanging off the side and looking down below at the water banging and bashing up froth. There was money to be made for a boy in Bay Center. You could pick berries or strip bark off of trees. Stripping the bark off of trees was great for kids. We would make a long cut in the bark with a knife, then put our fingers beneath the edge of the cut bark and push our hand around the tree, stripping off the bark as we went. A day's effort would fill a wagon with bark, which could be sold for a couple of dollars at the country store—a fair amount of spending money for a boy in the 1950s.

There was a lot to do in Bay Center. Kids then had much more freedom than they do these days. Friends and I would spend our free time exploring the town and the harbor and its surroundings. We hiked up and down the river, walked to the beach and out into the bay, picked berries, fished, and, of course, stripped bark. I remember it being a fun place to be.

Mom was very impressed with the natural beauty of Bay Center, the surrounding area and the coast, in general. She was amazed by the way everything grew so easily. "You can plant anything here and it just grows and grows. Nebraska is not like that. I guess it is all the rain here." But she still said, "There's nothing more beautiful than a field of wheat blowing in the wind."

Mom still tried to teach me things. One day she saw me brushing crumbs off the kitchen table onto the floor. She said firmly, "Don't do that, don't ever do that. That's shanty." That resulted in a discussion of shanty Irish, who were poor Irish who didn't appropriately clean up their homes or themselves. You don't ever want to be shanty; they are Irish who disgrace the rest of us.

She also mentioned "lace curtain Irish," who were apparently some Irish who had a little money and put on airs as if they were something special, better than other Irish. Both shanty and lace curtain Irish were derogatory terms for some Irish, often used by the Irish themselves.

She really wanted me to play the piano, but that was impossible since we moved so much from town to town. I tried the clarinet in Paisley but that didn't work out, so in Bay Center, she bought me a very nice accordion and scheduled me for weekly lessons in South Bend, a town twenty miles away. I tried it for a few years but never was much good. I should have known music was not for me. I cannot carry a tune at all. My first clue was in Toppenish. While practicing for a church production of some sort, Father Funari said that Sammy Rodriquez and I should "sing softly, very, very softly." I knew Sammy couldn't sing. As time when on, I realized that I could not sing well either, but the final blow was one evening when Mari (my daughter) was little and I was trying to sing her to sleep; she looked up at me and said, "No sing, Daddy, no sing." That was the end of my singing. Incidentally, years later when I mentioned my lack of singing ability to Pat, she said, "Oh, I can't carry a tune at all either." Maybe it is familial. Her husband Dick, my brother-in-law, had a beautiful tenor voice and sang in the church choir for years.

One friend from Bay Center stands out in my memory. Mel Frank was a big kid and an Indian. He used to keep seals as pets in a pen in his backyard. I'm sure he let them out to visit the ocean, but I remember being fascinated by the sight of those two seals, grunting and flopping around in his yard the same way my relatives probably kept pigs in Nebraska. Mel also defended me from local bullies. Being one of the biggest kids our age, they listened when he told them to "leave the new kid alone." I appreciated his help and his friendship. Years later, I went back to Bay Center and stopped by his house to see if I could tell him that. His brother told me that Mel now worked for the Washington State Forestry Department. I wish I had gotten his number and passed on my thanks.

For the first year or so that Mom and I lived in Bay Center, we rented a little house with no indoor plumbing on a side road. There was an outhouse and a slop bucket to be used during the night. I was pretty impressed by the idea that we could just use a bucket instead of going outside.

Our landlord, Mr. Rhodes, was an older guy who walked with a limp and was missing most fingers on his right hand. He was kind, but was completely different from me. Mr. Rhodes gifted me an old dump car that wasn't running and had been sitting in his backyard. He thought it was a wonderful present for a boy my age. "Take it apart! Put it back together! Do anything you want!" he proclaimed with a grin. I wouldn't touch it. Couldn't care less about tinkering with an old car. The poor man just couldn't understand why I wouldn't take him up on his generous offer.

Probably unrelated to the rejected car, Mom and I moved to a different rental in a big garage full of crab pots. Three-fourths of the garage was full of fishing equipment: boats, nets, crab pots... In the back, there was a teeny tiny apartment that we lived in. Though it was small, it had a bathroom. So, we thought of it as a move up in the world. Mom liked it, I remember. It was smaller, but cleaner than the other house. And indoor plumbing makes a big difference in your life.

That landlord was also generous. Whenever he had a good run of crabs, he would toss a couple at our door and leave them there in a little box. Mom, knowing she could never afford to buy them at the market, would lecture me: "This is really special. Crabs are special stuff. They're really good."

I think Mom wanted to think of herself and her family as cultivated, and that we were the kind of people who appreciated the finer things in life. For some reason, it was very important to her to rise above her circumstances. I don't know for certain, but I think she wanted more for herself in life. When that didn't happen, she wanted more for me instead. So, there in our tiny apartment in the back of a boat garage lit by kerosene lamps, Mom taught me to very carefully break the crabs apart and eat them daintily in a sort of ceremony of gratitude and hope. Mom would say, "This is really—you know, people pay a lot of money for these crabs."

Hope for a better life was Mom's aspiration, but the Catholic Church and her faith were the foundation she stood upon. She was a gentle Catholic. By that I mean that she believed in God and in people being decent to one another. I think just teaching school and raising a son was all she could handle. Her message to me was, "Be nice to people. Be kind and expect the same in return. And go to church." Having the church in her life provided a beacon for her to move toward. Weekly services and special holidays provided the rituals that made our lives more meaningful. That's probably why we almost died trying to get to Christmas mass one year.

The first winter we lived in Bay Center, Mom decided we would attend Midnight Mass in a nearby town since Bay Center had no Catholic church. The journey involved driving through the night at the edge of the water on a road that was paved with loose crushed oyster shells. (There's an oyster cannery in Bay Center. The discarded shells were crushed and used on the roads instead of gravel.) This was the road we used to access the highway.

Christmas Eve we got our dressy clothes on, climbed in the car and, despite the nervousness of the dangers and the driving, we set off for mass. But the fog had rolled in from the bay. We couldn't see in front of the car at all, and there was no painted yellow line on that service road. Mom said, "Joe, you get out and walk in front of the car to find the way." So, out I went into the chilly humidity. The night air was clammy and wet on my face. Our '49 Chevy's headlights refracted light off the mist. Rather than illuminating the road, the light diffused and cast a hazy glow on everything and nothing at the same time. It was tough going without linear posts or road markings to use as guides.

Finally, we gave up and turned back. "Too dangerous," Mom said. "And we'll have enough trouble getting back home as it is." I remember being impressed with my mom's determination to go to mass. We went quite a ways in the night fog, and she hated driving even in the best conditions.

Christmas time for me is full of happy memories. Mom decorated wherever we lived with lights and tinsel on the walls. She hung a wreath up, but didn't bother with a tree since there was usually one in her schoolroom and that was probably more than she could handle. Her rule for expending effort was to do everything she had to and not much more. That was okay with me. I didn't (and still don't) notice things like décor.

I do remember anticipating two cardboard boxes that came in the mail every Christmas. I couldn't wait to get the presents from both Pat and Peg. In all those different towns, their boxes still found me. It made me feel noticed and special. I would have been heartbroken if I didn't get them. Every year, I would shout, "Here's the box!" Inside each present were sweaters and clothes and things I didn't care about much, but it was okay. I just loved the packages for what they represented. They served as an anchor in an unfamiliar place, a signal that I was remembered and loved by my family. And for Peg, that effort was above and beyond. She had gotten married and moved to California and later to St. Louis. Although we wrote letters, she wasn't in close contact with the family. I always appreciated the extra effort she took to remember the baby boy she once knew.

While in Bay Center, Mom got some sort of certification that made her eligible to teach as a certified teacher in the state of Washington. The other two teachers in the three-room school were a husband and wife, the Broders. I especially liked Mr. Broder. He was the principal. He was my kind of teacher. In class, he liked to put his feet up on his desk, lean back in his chair, and for long periods of time he would read easy fractions and equations that we worked out on the blackboard. Also, the bells that rang to start and end school or recess were not automatic. He would ring them whenever he felt like it. This often resulted in remarkably long recesses and lunch times, which all the students, and probably also my mother, appreciated.

They apparently liked Mom and wanted her to stay in Bay Center now that her world of possibilities had opened up and she could go anywhere. They said, "Cecilia, you don't want to go to those big cities and have to go along with all those rules. You should just stay here in Bay Center now that you've got a certificate." But she got two job offers, the first time she had ever had a choice in where to go. Up until this point, Mom had been lucky to get any offer at all. We usually moved right before the school year was set to start. This year she had to make a decision.

Chapter 3

Secondary School

I - Toppenish

Mom was thrilled to have two job offers to choose from. The first offer was in a town called Toppenish on the Yakama Indian Reservation in Washington State. The second was in Omak, Washington in the Cascade Mountains. One town had a Catholic school and one didn't. Even though she was proud that she and Dad were public school teachers, sending me to Catholic school was important to Mom. So, she picked the town with that amenity.

Off we went to the "big city" of Toppenish, population 5,000. I remember right after we got to town, Mom and I had lunch in the Huba Huba Café. Enjoying my drink, I gazed out the big front window and was surprised see Indians! There they were, just walking up and down the street! Brown skin, long hair, different facial structure. Somehow, they looked even more Indian than Mel Frank and the Indians that I had known at Bay Center. Mom noticed too and then abruptly changed the subject. She had something else on her mind.

"I gotta tell you something, Joe. It turns out I got confused. The Catholic school is in Omak. I chose the wrong town, so you're gonna be going to Toppenish Junior High." I always thought that was funny. Sending me to Catholic school was her number one reason for leaving Bay Center, and she picked the town without a Catholic school.

If ever there was a woman whose life could have been improved by Google, my mom was it.

The city of Toppenish sits just inside the Yakama Indian reservation, but is run separately from the reservation. It's a bit confusing, actually. The Toppenish city limits weren't (and still aren't) considered part of the reservation. So, although it served an American Indian population, the city's government and services of Toppenish were not directed by the tribe. There were also other schools on the reservation that Indians attended. This separation meant that I saw Indians around town, but didn't have many interactions with them personally.

Toppenish sits in the Yakima Valley in central Washington. Because of the nearby river and the protection from the mountains, soil there is fertile and temperatures are temperate, which makes it an ideal place to grow fruit. The Yakima wine industry that thrives there now had its start in the early 1900s. Since it was settled, there have been grapes and other crops like apples and hops growing there that needed harvesting. Those industries drew a migrant Hispanic population, some of whom settled there as well. So, long story short, Toppenish is racially diverse.

Even though I had lots of experience at meeting new people, I wasn't the best at making new friends. It's still hard for me to do that. I'm pretty insecure. Like most people, I'm afraid they'll find out that I'm really not that good, which I understand is actually very common in humans. One reassurance I had in school was that I felt I was smart. I don't mean to be arrogant, but that was a very reassuring thing to have that leg to stand on. I knew that at least I would do pretty well in school.

I went to Toppenish Junior High School in seventh and eighth grade. I was nervous starting yet another new school. So, when George Long sat down next to me in my first class and said, "You're new here, right?" I breathed a sigh of relief. We've been friends ever since. He was a brilliant student. He went on to work for the Navy in rocketry. We still see each other every now and then. I remember one time he was telling me something about work and I said, "George, don't worry about it, it isn't rocket science." And then we looked at each other and I said, "You're a rocket scientist, aren't you?" And then we laughed. George and his wife Martha live in Virginia.

I spent a lot of time at George's house and always had great respect for his mother, who really helped raise me. She also worked at Safeway and she was always cheerful, generous and kind.

In Toppenish, I made great friends that I have kept to this day. I think being able to stay in one place for more than one or two years really made a difference for me. I lived in Toppenish until I went to college and my mother stayed for ten more years after that. Even now, when people ask where I'm from, I say Toppenish. I want to mention a few of those lifelong friends here.

Jim Strom was a friend from those times who I still see from time to time. He and his wife, Linda, came to Omaha recently and we went to a couple of Creighton Big East basketball games. He and Linda taught school and he coached basketball for decades in Okanogan, Washington in the Cascade Mountains. Jim and I played various sports together but he was always more athletic than me. He could run, do the hurdles, swim and play basketball better than me. I was always jealous. They now live in Liberty Lake, Washington. Another friend, Bob Massong, really loved cars and still does. His father owned a bakery and spoke with a German accent, but I don't think Bob wanted to work as hard as a baker like his father had to. I don't blame him. Bob and his wife Anne live in Yakima, where he was a parole officer. Larry Elder is another friend from those days. Larry took over the family farm and eventually decided to grow grapes in addition to corn, thus becoming a part of the Yakima Valley wine movement. Larry and I got in a fistfight once. He hit me a couple of times and I said, "Okay, you win," and I quit. Larry and I talked about the fight at a recent Toppenish high school reunion. He laughed and said, "I couldn't figure out why you quit." Well, I know why, and I still think it was one of my better decisions. He was a tough farm kid.

Before I got to know all those guys very well, I had a weird experience. Our first residence in town was a place called Red Gables. It was an apartment building for teachers' housing. One day, Mom sent me upstairs to have Mr. Edwards teach me how to properly knot a necktie. He showed me how to do that and then disappeared. When he came back, he had his pajamas on and wanted to wrestle on the bed. I was scared to death. I was 11 years old and had no idea what was going on, only knew that this felt very scary and wrong. Then he wanted to stare into my eyes. That's when the creepiness of the situation became too much and I just left without saying anything to him. It seemed like things could have gone further, and I'm glad I left when I did. I never told a soul about that, though I eventually found out from my friends that Mr. Edwards was known to be attracted to boys. It seemed to be common knowledge. They all told him to buzz off in one way or another. My mother would have died to hear about that. I certainly never told her. It was just one of the many things I had to figure out for myself. I never went into his apartment again.

I enjoyed my time in Toppenish Junior High very much. It was nice to finally be rooted somewhere and have friends that I could count on seeing. Mom, however, still held out hope that I would get that Catholic education. When I was nearing the end of eighth grade, I came home one day and my mom was waiting for me with a priest. He was from St. Martin's High School in Olympia, Washington, a Benedictine Catholic boarding school. He was there to help her make the case for aiming a little higher in my studies. I wasn't failing junior high, but I wasn't excelling either. Sometimes I was a goofball in class and my grades showed it.

Mom didn't want to push academics too hard; I think in part, she was tired and just didn't have the energy to make sure I got my homework done, but also she wanted me to be self-reliant. She loved learning and probably hoped that I would love it too, but I had to come to it on my own. Mom and the priest suggested that a private high school would offer more opportunity than the school in Toppenish, better academics, and of course, religious instruction.

After he left, Mom said I had three options. I could go to boarding school at St. Martin's. I could travel twenty miles away each day to attend the Jesuit high school in Yakima. Or I could move to Omaha, live with Pat's family and attend Creighton Prep High School. My preference would have been Toppenish High School with my friends, but that wasn't one of the options. I really didn't want to move away from Toppenish where my friends (and my mother) were. I argued a little bit, but generally accepted my mother's edict. So, I picked the Jesuit high school in Yakima called Marquette.

I lived with my mother, kept my Toppenish friends (many for the rest of my life) and commuted into Yakima for high school. I had a very good experience with the Jesuits. I think Mom was correct in her guess that it would be good for me. Maybe Marquette *was* a little more rigorous academically than Toppenish High, but I do think "Top-Hi" was a good school with superb teachers. It's hard to argue about the quality of a high school that produced a future rocket scientist like George Long. Also, the principal at Toppenish High School was Jim Strom's father, a wonderful man, loved and respected by all.

I wasn't always sure what my mother felt about me. I knew she loved me, but I didn't realize how proud she was of my academic ability until the day she took me to meet the principal of Marquette High School. She explained to him with some pride that I should be a good student because my records (meaning my IQ test) were excellent. Though my grades were average, she indicated to him that I had untapped potential.

When school started for ninth grade, Mom arranged for me to catch a ride to a school bus stop every morning with a fine man named Joseph Murphy, a lawyer in Toppenish. He drove his own family the few miles to the bus stop every day and I was able to ride along with them. Mr. Murphy always listened to the news on the radio, which I thought was kind of interesting. The bus ride into Yakima took about half an hour. We arrived at Marquette High School around 8:00 every day and got to work.

II – Marquette & the Jesuits

When I walked up those steps to enter the old stone building (The Rock) housing Marquette High School in the fall of 1955, I began a relationship with the Society of Jesus—the Jesuits)—that would last well over 50 years. The Society of Jesus is the largest order of priests and brothers in the Catholic Church, numbering nearly 17,000. It is not the purpose of this book to describe the Jesuits in detail, but considering their impact on my education, my career, and my life, I think some comments are appropriate.

In 2000, Peter-Hans Kolvenback, S.J., at that time the Superior General of the Society of Jesus, spoke at Creighton University. He can describe the Jesuit Mission in education better than I.

"The Society of Jesus proclaims that the service of faith through the promotion of justice is the mission that must be integrated as a priority into each Jesuit work.

"Our purpose in education, then, is to form men and women 'for others.' The Society of Jesus has always sought to imbue students with values that transcend the goals of money, fame, and success. We want graduates who will be leaders concerned about society and the world in which they live. We want graduates who desire to eliminate hunger and conflict in the world and who are sensitive to the need for more equitable distribution of the world's goods. We want graduates who seek to end sexual and social discrimination and who are eager to share their faith with others.

"In short, we want our graduates to be leaders-in-service. That has been the goal of Jesuit education since the sixteenth century. It remains so today."

In many ways, Marquette was an unusual Jesuit school. With an enrollment of approximately 200 boys, it was the smallest of the 60 Jesuit high schools in the United States. I doubt that it was "selective" in admissions at all. We didn't have a gymnasium; our football field was a couple of miles away. Amenities such as shop or band or hot lunch didn't exist. We were adjacent to St. Joseph Church and grade school, and one block away from St. Joseph's Academy for girls. The grounds, limited as they were, were paved, with minimal grass.

Dress code included white shirts with long sleeves and we were often reminded how fortunate we were that students no longer had to wear ties. Due to the school's small size, only two foreign languages were taught, French and Latin. Again, we were reminded how fortunate we were that we no longer had to learn Greek. This was pre-Vatican II, and mass and many prayers were still in Latin. So, unfortunately, I took four years of Latin. By the fourth year there were only seven students left in my Latin class.

Since the Jesuits were founded by St. Ignatius of Loyola (Spain), in 1534, they have been loved, hated, and even feared at times. In my opinion, those who have been most hostile have generally had very limited actual knowledge of the Jesuits, and often are expressing their hostility toward the Catholic Church itself. In reality, the Society of Jesus has had a very limited role in church leadership. Jesuits prefer not to be bishops or cardinals. The only Jesuit ever to be elected pope was Pope Francis in 2013. In recent years, the Jesuits have been more recognized for what they, hopefully, really are, men attempting to lead holy lives and to be of service to others by living Jesuit values. Historically, they have been scholars, educators (with 28 universities and colleges in the USA and over 160 worldwide), missionaries and martyrs, researchers, inventors, linguists, and advisors to royalty and governments. They take vows of poverty, chastity, and obedience, and are expected to be "men for others" demonstrating a "special option" for the poor.

To be a Jesuit priest, a man must undergo 11 or 12 years of study, teaching, and prayer before ordination. During these years of preparation, he is called a scholastic. He may wear the usual clerical dress, including the black robes, and is addressed simply as Mister. After ordination he becomes a priest and is called Father.

When I entered Marquette we had five priests, six scholastics and two lay teachers. Today, there are fewer Jesuits throughout the world and the large majority of teachers in Jesuit schools are lay faculty. It is imperative that all faculty understand and be supportive of the Jesuit mission in education, if there is to be any hope in continuing the schools and programs successfully.

There are many wonderful organizations of men and women in the world, some Catholic, many not, some Christian, many not. The Society of Jesus is one of them and the one that I am most familiar with. I believe that organizations that emphasize and promote knowledge, thoughtfulness, honesty, compassion, and good works, are worthwhile and needed in the world. I do not wish my affection and respect for the Society of Jesus to imply exclusivity. I just wish to explain why it has had such an effect on my life.

With my less-than-stellar grades and habits of studying, the world of Marquette came as kind of a shock. I admit that I thought I was a pretty smart guy (I'm humble too). School hadn't challenged me much, so I had developed the habit of sitting in the back, daydreaming and sort of half paying attention. Basically, I was lazy about school.

After doing this for a few months with the Jesuits, Mister Cronin, a Jesuit scholastic, got fed up with me. He backed me up against a wall between classes.

"You make me sick! I have looked at your potential (IQ scores) and your class performance scores and you make me sick!" he said. "You don't study. You're not even trying. You could be somebody, but you are not going to amount to anything. You just make me sick."

I remember thinking but not saying out loud, "I'm not real fond of you either."

I was angry and embarrassed, but the conversation with Mister Cronin stuck with me. It got me thinking that I might need to try harder. And it scared me into behaving a bit better, at least when he was watching.

Another scholastic had the same observations, but he tried a different approach that worked better with me. Mister Morisette walked into English class one day and said to me, "Lynch, I know your record. I know everything about you, and you are simply an A student. I know that. So I've already given you the grade for the semester. You have an A. Now let's go to work."

I loved it. The friendliness, and assurance that I could, in fact, get an A...it helped motivate me to work harder. I wasn't the greatest student ever, but I certainly tried hard for him. At the semester's end Mister Morisette handed me my report card and said, "I told you you're an A student." (This was back when a "B" was considered a good grade, long before today's grade inflation.) When I graduated from Marquette, he signed my annual: "Now that we have you moving, keep moving!" I liked him; he spent the rest of his life teaching at Gonzaga University and died a few years ago.

I can't say that high school helped me completely reform my immature ways all at once. I still think of myself as a little immature, and I'm well into my seventies. But bit by bit, mister by mister, the Jesuits helped me take my studies a bit more seriously. They kept saying I had potential, and I came to believe it. I loved them for helping me recognize that in myself. They also taught me to be a bit more thoughtful. One day, after a tough exam, I complained to my teacher, a young scholastic. I said, "This course will never be useful or helpful in life. What value does it have? Why do we have to take it?" Mister Neumann looked up from his desk and said softly and slowly, "To become an educated man." I thought about his reply quite a bit. I still think about it. It was a great answer, a great reason to study and learn. Even then, I understood and agreed with him.

As I mentioned, my first year at Marquette, Joseph Murphy took me with his family to catch a school bus to Yakima each morning. The next year, I caught a ride every morning with a man named Roy Bush. He lived in Toppenish and taught school in Yakima, and would drop me off at Marquette. Mom and I met him when he was the leader of my Boy Scout troop. He was a convert to Catholicism. Each morning, he pulled out the rosary; we said it on the way to Yakima. I kept hoping he would forget, but he never did. Mr. Bush also taught CCD to the public school kids. One time he invited me to go to that class, thinking that I would be a good example, lifelong Catholic that I was. He told me later that he was sorry he invited me because I was not at all well behaved. I giggled and made fun in the back. Instead of being a role model, I was disruptive. I still feel badly about that.

III – Friends in Toppenish

As I proceeded through high school at Marquette, I loved the atmosphere and the teachers (even Mister Cronin), and became more successful academically, but my social life never bloomed. I never really felt that I fit in with the other students, most of whom had gone to grade school together and lived in Yakima. I just felt like I was a kid from Toppenish, on the reservation. At the end of the school day, I went home to my friends in Toppenish.

I tried to play basketball at Marquette, with limited success. Since the school was so small no one who tried out for the team was "cut," so I made the team, but it turned out to be quite a hassle. After practice, I had to walk to the Greyhound Bus station where I had to wait for a bus to Toppenish, which was awkward and time consuming to say the least. A couple of winters during basketball season, I was able to live in Yakima some of the time with the Ibach family, Dick and Bill, classmates, who were very kind to me.

My senior year a couple of friends asked me to join the Toppenish CYO (Catholic Youth Organization) basketball team. The Marquette team basketball season had already started but I certainly was not playing regularly, and I would get to play a lot more with the CYO team because it wasn't as good. So I quit the Marquette team and was genuinely surprised that the coach seemed disappointed or even annoyed at me. I thought he would be happy to get rid of me. Anyway, the CYO team did well; I got to play more and had a couple of good games. We even made a tournament in Seattle. I enjoyed it.

One year I was on the track team at Marquette and we had a track meet in Toppenish. I was running the 440-yard dash, which is an awful race. I knew I wasn't very good, but I didn't want to be embarrassed there. As we lined up for the start, Larry Elder, who was running for Toppenish High and could run like the wind, said, "Joe, just fall in right behind me and stay with me." Well, I tried, but by the end of the first turn he was somewhere up ahead, out of my sight. I remember there were three of us at the back. I gave it all I had, determined not to finish last. I think I finished sixth or seventh out of eight, and I was okay with that. I don't recall how Larry did but he probably won the race.

Sometimes friends and I went to concerts at the National Guard Armory in Yakima. There weren't many seats; the crowd mostly just stood on the gym floor, the same gym floor that Marquette played its home basketball games on. Yakima was often a stop for shows that were on the road from Spokane to Seattle or Portland. I saw Sam Cooke there before he was very famous. When Jerry Lee Lewis came, he managed to introduce himself, play the piano with his hands, his feet, while lying on top of the piano, and while lying on the floor, say goodbye and get off the stage, all in 20 minutes. I was not very impressed. My favorite, by far, was Fats Domino. He came out, on time, said nothing, just nodded his head to the crowd, sat down at the piano and softly and slowly began singing, "I'm walkin' to New Orleans…" He sang over two hours without stopping, stood up and said thanks and walked off the stage. Even at the time, I thought it was special, and I still do. The next year he came again but he didn't sing nearly as long. I guess he just felt like singing that first evening. There was a local group we liked too, "The Checkers." They looked good, moving back and forth together with their sport coats and saxophones. We almost never had girlfriends or dates; we just liked the music. As I recall, admission was $2.00. My favorite song was "Louie, Louie," by the Kingsmen, out of Seattle, which is still heard today. The Kingsmen never had another hit.

Mostly I hung out with the guys like George Long and Jim Strom. We played baseball or wandered around until the streetlights came on. Occasionally, we would throw water balloons at cars or lean a two-pound coffee can full of water against a door and ring the doorbell and run. We quit that one evening when a man burst out the door just as we rang the doorbell and caught us. He just said, "Knock it off" and we did. We got into various scrapes, but no major trouble. There was a bit of beer drinking, though we were underage. I remember my friends and I would take a case of Oly (Olympia beer) out to a gravel pit on the reservation, and sit around drinking and quizzing each other on sports.

When you got legally old enough to drink, you could get a state-issued ID card, which we called an "Oly card." But before we were 21, the inflexible Washington State legal drinking age, we had to get creative about acquiring beer. It helped that I had a job at a grocery store.

When I was 15 or 16, I started working at Safeway in Toppenish. George Long was working there and recommended me for the job. (The manager at Safeway asked him if he knew anyone who was as good a worker as him, and he recommended me. It always helps to have friends.) It was a great job. I learned a lot about self-reliance and work ethic. The work schedule was posted each week and I never knew how many hours I would get, but I—and everyone else—always hoped for as many as possible. I needed the money for my shenanigans and I helped Mom with expenses too. But about the beer...

There were a number of underage employees at Safeway who worked together to get Oly. One guy would grab some beer and set it behind a counter. Someone else would bag it up and take it out with the garbage. Another person would drive up behind the store and pick it up. I'm not proud of this behavior. At the time, we thought we were so clever, but I can see now what a betrayal of my manager's trust this was. I had it in my mind at the time that if we got caught we'd probably just get warned, but I doubt if that is true. I think management would have said, "It's over," and fired all of us. Liquor laws in the state of Washington were very tight. There were no alcohol sales on Sundays. No one under 21 was permitted to buy alcohol. Period. If our smuggling ring of underage employees had been discovered, our theft and law violation would have left the store manager with no recourse but to fire every single one of us. And what a loss that would have been for me.

Safeway was where I really learned to work hard. I worked two or three summers there and during all the vacations during the school year. Sometimes on a school break, I would work all night when the store was closed. I enjoyed that solitude. I would turn the radio up full blast, mop the floors, stock the shelves, and carry out the garbage—the actual garbage. Safeway was also where I encountered more of the racial diversity of Toppenish.

One night after the store was closed and I was working alone, I was outside on a tall ladder changing lights on the side of the store. A car pulled up by my ladder and some Mexican guys got out and started saying things: "What are you doing up there? Why don't you come down and we'll see how tough you are." I said, "Well, I am working here, you know..." I was afraid of them and tried to say I was busy. Then the shadowy figure that had gotten out of the car last came into focus. This muscular, dark-skinned guy who appeared to be leading the crew was none other than Joey Garcia. I knew Joey. We played some CYO basketball together. We went to junior high together and got on pretty well. Our eyes met and I could see he recognized me too. The other guys were amping up their volume and aggression. It seemed like they were going to beat the living daylights out of me if they could just get me off that ladder. I was getting very nervous when suddenly Joey said loudly, "Let the motherfucker go, we don't give a shit about him. Let's go!" The other guys stopped, looked at Joey, then got in the car and drove off. I never saw Joey again, but I understood what he had done, and I was very grateful.

IV - Race

The thing about Toppenish was that even though there were Mexicans, whites, and Yakama Indians all through the town, everyone kept pretty much to their own groups. I didn't really understand at the time that the white population considered the Mexicans as lesser.

I never thought of them as non-white. But Joey knew. He had been dating a white girl, but her parents wouldn't allow it. Eventually, Joey's girlfriend got shipped off to a boarding school in Seattle to break them up. He was a good guy who lived in a time and place where he wasn't allowed to rise beyond his station. That night in the alley, Joey artfully tiptoed through the narrow territory between protecting his white friend and keeping his allegiance to his crew. The experience scared the pants off of me. It can't have been much easier for Joey.

If circumstances were tough in town for the Mexicans, the Yakama Indians had it worse. Even though we technically lived on their reservation, there was a lot of prejudice against them. Some people called them "fat cheeks" due to their facial structure. (The Yakamas supposedly have higher cheekbones, and therefore show a bit more cheek than people of European descent.) Among the "righteous" residents of Toppenish, the Yakamas were considered lower than the Mexicans.

Even my stalwart and solitary mother got riled up about race every now and then in Toppenish. We rented from a family of Mexicans who were permanent residents, the Cernas. They were well-respected farmers. Mom loved them. One day, people looking to buy the house next door stopped by our house to ask about the neighborhood. The man speaking had an accent that I didn't recognize. They asked incredulously if Mexicans really owned our home.

Mom said, "Yes."

Then they asked, "Are they ever around here?"

The insinuation was that they would be less interested in buying if we answered yes. I could see Mom's color rising. She responded, "Any time they want!" and slammed the door. As she walked across the room, she said "damn Dutchman." That was very unusual behavior for my mother. I had no idea what Dutchman meant, so I asked her. She explained to me that, "those Germans with their accent are implying that the Cernas are less than them." She didn't like that. Mom didn't exactly campaign for minority equal rights, but she thought people should be kind to one another, no matter their race or religion. She didn't have time for intolerance. And she gave her loyalty to people who treated her with kindness and respect.

One of my mother's closest friends, another schoolteacher, was Indian (Shoshone) and Mom would notice things. She told me, "You can always tell someone who has had some education by how they treat people, just like you can tell a quality restaurant. Last week when we had dinner at the Four Winds in Yakima, they were so nice to Mary Jo, they treated her just like anyone else."

I am not sure at all that so-called "educated people" necessarily demonstrate much benefit from their education, but maybe she had a point about quality restaurants.

At school, Mom had many more Hispanic kids than whites in her second-grade classroom. I know she did her best to be fair, though working with the migrant children was hard. They were very challenging to teach. They had to move with the harvest, so she might have them for a couple of months and then not see them again until the following year. Many of them only spoke Spanish. And this was long before ESL programs existed in schools. She just had to make do with her own experience and resources. So, when they would tell her their names, sometimes she would rename them. I understand that this would not be acceptable today, but this was 1950-something. Mom didn't speak any Spanish, and she didn't have a teacher's aide, a translator, or a literacy specialist. So if a name was too hard to understand or if she thought other kids would tease them, she would say, "How about Bill. We'll go with Bill."

Then she would assign Bill a friend because he didn't speak or read English and needed a guide. "Bill, you and Bennie are best friends now. You will be friends forever." Her methods seemed to work. The kids wanted to make friends. And the two new buddies would set about trying to learn each other's languages. If the new kid stayed for more than a semester, he learned English and could pretty much keep up with the class discussion.

I think growing up in Toppenish shaped the way I look at the world. I still try to carry with me Mom's example of gentle Catholicism. I try to be patient, which is not easy for me, to be compassionate, to be of service to others. I think people should be nice to each other. I think we should work for the common good and care for the less fortunate. I'm frustrated that a lot of people don't seem to care.

If I had to boil my worldview down to a sentence or two, I would quote an esteemed teacher I once heard lecture. The man started his talk by saying, "I believe everybody wants to make something of their life, and that is the basis of my teaching." I have remembered that forever because that's a good foundation for a teacher and a caretaker to start with. I would add, "But they can be defeated and lose that desire." I do believe that all people want to be more, and if they have an opportunity they will try.

I want to record one other memory from my high school years that might be of interest to modern-day readers. Up until we lived in Toppenish, Mom and I did not own a television. In Bay Center, we sometimes went over to the neighbor's house to watch college basketball games. I thought that was great fun, actually.

After I had started high school, Mom came home one day and said, "We're getting a TV. All my students are talking about what's on TV, and I don't know anything about it." She thought she should probably keep up with the second-graders she was teaching.

I can't remember everything we watched. Many nights, I was outside with my friends, but I can recall watching *The Ed Sullivan Show* with Elvis. I thought it was weird that they didn't show anything below his waist and just focused on his face.

I graduated from Marquette in 1959. I was thinking of going to college. Mom wanted that for me, and I could see from my own working experiences that life might be easier if I had a degree. I hadn't decided on a school yet. But the Jesuits had goals for me. In July, I got a letter from Gonzaga University in Spokane, saying they had a recommendation for a partial scholarship for me, but no application. They wanted to know, "Are you coming?" I wrote back and said, "If I have a scholarship I am coming." I never found out which of my Jesuit teachers help me get that recommendation, but I was pleased and considered it a compliment.

I had been disappointed at graduation. I had hoped to be offered some help for college. The valedictorian, who was also our student body president, was joining the Jesuits. The salutatorian received a scholarship to Seattle University, and the student who ranked behind me received a scholarship to St. Martin's College. I was ranked third out of forty-four and had managed to get elected student body vice president; I also felt I met the financial needs guidelines. Needless to say, I was very happy to receive a scholarship offer, especially to Gonzaga, even if it was only partial.

So, it looked like even though Mom picked the wrong town for Catholic education, she got her wish after all. Not only did I attend a Jesuit high school, I was heading for more Catholic-inspired teaching as an undergraduate at Gonzaga.

Maybe Mom mixed up Toppenish and Omak, didn't drive a car very well, and wasn't much of a cook, but sometimes she could say things that really made me think. After years of refusing to relate to my questions and harassment about whether she was a Democrat or a Republican, one evening she said, "Well, I don't understand politics or politicians very well, but the Democrats seem to care more about poor people, and we have always been poor." So, I guess we were Democrats, as most Irish Catholics were in those days. She added that sometimes, if she didn't know who to vote for, she would just vote for women or for the Irish names. I told her that didn't sound very logical to me and she said, "Oh, I'm just balancing out the people who go through voting against women and the Irish names."

Once, while we were traveling, we went to mass and the priest had a thick Irish accent. I mentioned how beautiful it sounded. She said, "He's probably just one of those Irish priests who stands in front of the mirror each morning practicing his brogue so he doesn't lose it."

Other words of wisdom from Mom:

- "If someone says that money is not important, they have never been without it."
- "I don't know why both my girls wanted to marry doctors' sons. At least they have good English." Mom was very tired of being told how fortunate it was that her girls were both marrying doctors' sons. Mom felt strongly that Pat and Peg were the special ones and deserved the most attention, not their husbands-to-be.
- She once told me, "You don't have to answer all Sister Marceline's (my aunt) letters if you don't want to, you know." That seemed out of character for Mom, giving permission for me not to have to answer letters. Later, I decided Mom really just wanted to be sure that there was no pressure on me to be a priest.
- One day when I was home from medical school, Mom asked me, "Why are all the doctors against old people getting medical care?" I didn't understand why she would say something

like that, but later I understood. In the 1960s the debate about "healthcare for the elderly" (Medicare) was going on. Mom had read that the president of the American Medical Association (AMA) had stated, "Healthcare is a privilege, not a right," and that the AMA was totally against any form of Medicare. Even at Creighton, during my sophomore year, the chairman of Pathology, a good man whom the students respected very much, spent one entire class sitting on his desk and explaining to us, very earnestly, why Medicare was a very bad idea. I loved him as a man and a teacher, but I did not believe him then and don't believe him now. He did save me a lot of money in AMA dues. I never joined the AMA until decades later when it changed its stance. As usual, Mom was right.

- One of the most beautiful things about growing old is all the wonderful memories.

Chapter 4

Gonzaga University

I – Becoming a Freshman, Fall 1959

Mom gave me one of her rare hugs. I was walking out the door, preparing to go from Toppenish to Spokane for my freshman year at Gonzaga. Its suddenness startled me. Hugs were usually reserved for birthdays and funerals. Since embraces were so rare between us, they were usually stiff and awkward, but always memorable.

She said, "If it doesn't work out you can always come back. Don't worry about it." I remember thinking, *Why wouldn't it work out?* What a peacock I was. At age 17, I didn't know what I didn't know. But Mom did, and she wanted to reassure me that I had safe harbor with her.

I found that I liked college. I stayed in De Smet Hall, the freshman dorm at Gonzaga. I wasn't very independent, so I was happy to have access to a cafeteria where the food was much better than Mom's cooking. I liked that my schedule was structured. I had a lot to do, but I still had down time. And I looked forward to letters from Mom telling me she was proud of me, and what she was doing. Those letters also included checks because she continued to support me financially.

University-level work was challenging for me. I wanted to do well, but it wasn't that easy for me. Arriving the first year they gave us a math test. There were 40 questions, and if you got 30 right, you got put in an advanced calculus class. If you got less than 30, you were placed in the lower level. I answered exactly 30 questions correctly, which meant I was the dumbest kid in the advanced class. Just based on the speed of the classroom discussion, I could tell exactly where I was compared to the others, and that was a revelation to me. I'd always been one of the smarter kids in my classes. Seeing those truly gifted mathematicians helped me see where my talents were...and where they weren't. I received a C in the advanced calculus course and I was very happy with it. Clearly, I wasn't cut out to be a mathematician, but it was the Sputnik era. There was enormous social pressure for the so-called smart kids to major in so-called "pure science" like engineering.

A little history is required to understand this pressure for patriotism's sake. In October 1957, the Soviets had launched a low-earth-orbit satellite. The U.S. was not even aware of the project until it launched. All of a sudden our best technology seemed small and poor by comparison. In December of the same year, our space program tried to launch the Vanguard TV3. It blew up two seconds after launch while the whole country was watching on television. There was a real worry that the Russians had exceeded us. Everyone thought our country had better get cracking if we were going to catch up and compete with them in what would eventually become the Cold War.

So there I was, a pimply teenager in calculus class, realizing that I was not cut out to be a chemical engineer. Those guys were the ones who would have enjoyed a car to take apart and put back together. That was how they spent their weekends. They were not just smart, they were *handy* and smart. I was not that. It became clear that I was not going to help design the U.S. version of Sputnik. So, for a semester I tried chemistry, figuring that if I couldn't build rockets, perhaps I could work on the reactions that fueled them. That lasted a semester. There were only eight students in my scientific chemistry class and one of the kids went on to become the head of the Hanford Atomic Works, the home of the first full-scale plutonium production reactor in the world. I didn't realize at the time that guy was a genius. I just thought I was dumb.

I felt kind of stuck. I knew from my high school job that working at Safeway would be a tough career. I didn't want to stand in a check stand or stock shelves every day, all day. I wasn't really good at fixing things. I didn't think I would be very good at selling insurance. Like most Catholic boys, I considered the priesthood, but that seemed awfully difficult. My mom said any degree is better than no degree, which was understandable considering her history. Plus, I could see she was correct. In order to find a job I would be good at, I was going to need a degree. So, I looked around, and there was the freshman dorm prefect, Father Tim O'Leary. He was the pre-med and pre-dental advisor for Gonzaga, and he suggested I take his organic chemistry class. So I did. And I found that I was pretty good at it. As time went on, I signed up for more classes like that one. Before I knew it, I was a declared pre-med major.

I ended up in pre-med studies not because I had been dreaming of being a doctor my whole life. Some people have that kind of drive. Not me. It took me a lot of wandering and changing direction to bounce into the area of study that matched my talents. I had detasseled corn, dug asparagus, picked peaches, apples and berries, peeled bark off of trees, tried to peg a hop field, and delivered newspapers. I worked at Safeway and drove tractors and trucks. I hunted pheasants and ducks and did many outdoor things as a senior patrol leader in Boy Scouts. For years, no matter what I tried, it seemed like others were always better. I feel like I stumbled accidentally into the career that became the rest of my life. Perhaps I can attribute some of that life path to mentors who were good at steering kids in the right direction. But also, I was lucky.

II – Seeing in Color

One other class that stands out from my freshman year was Psychology 101. When we reached the unit on vision and the brain, I made a startling discovery. In the textbook were some color-vision charts. They looked like circles with multicolored dots. In the center of some, I could see that the colored dots formed numbers. In others...nothing. It just looked like a page of dots. The professor stood in front of the classroom and said, "You should see a number three there." When I threw my hand up, kind of confused and worried, he said, "Just put it down until after class for God's sake. Come up then." Apparently this had happened to him before, and he had no patience or time for my jarring self-discovery.

I remember worrying for the rest of the period. After class, the professor pulled a book off his shelf and threw it at me, saying, "Look through there and tell me what numbers you see on those pages." I went all the way through, mystified. Page after page, I saw only dots. "I don't see any numbers." The professor paused his other conversation for a second and said, "You are red/green color-blind," and went on talking with the other students. As I wandered away from the classroom, I wondered to myself, "What is red/green color-blind?" I had no idea that color-blindness existed.

Through the years growing up, I had noticed that I wasn't seeing the same things other people were. My nieces and nephews at Pat's house used to tease me about colors. They would take out a stack of colored bowls from the kitchen and quiz me. That was sort of embarrassing, but as a kid I just figured I missed that material in school because I didn't go to kindergarten or first grade. Of course that line of thought doesn't hold up to scrutiny, but childhood explanations stick around until they're proven false: I had never really thought hard about what I could or could not see, and why that was different than other people.

Adding to the confusion, I can see some colors but not others. It is really a "color weakness," not a "color blindness." I can see blue and yellow, but not red and green. And blends with green and red in them tend to run together. So brown, tan, chartreuse (whatever that is) just appear the same to me. Most of the time, color-blindness isn't a big deal. It's not even unique. Eight to ten percent of American males are red/green color-blind, which adds up to over 10 million people in this country.

The issue only causes me trouble when I am dressing or driving. Wearing a weird color combination isn't dangerous, but driving through a red traffic light definitely is. I can remember as a young man wondering why everyone called the "white" traffic lights green. They look white to me. I kept track of them by their position on the light. I still try to be extra cautious when encountering a newer signal with more than three lights on it—or just a single light. Sometimes it can be difficult to tell a single blinking yellow light from a blinking red one. I drive slowly through those intersections.

Discovering the truth behind my color-blindness was a revelation to me. I finally understood that I wasn't "bad at colors." I just had a biological variation.

III – Shenanigans

As I said, I kind of liked dorm life. My freshman year, I stayed at De Smet Hall. As a sophomore, I was assigned to Welsh Hall. Part of my sophomore year, my roommate was Charles Braunger from Sioux City, Iowa. In 1966, I would marry his sister. Junior year, friends and I lived off campus in an apartment.

De Smet Hall was monitored by Father Tim O'Leary. My friends and I thought he was pretty grouchy and referred to him as Grim Tim. It was Father O'Leary's job to keep track of us freshmen. Most evenings his room door was open so he could see who was coming and going. That policy made the return from a night of partying a little perilous, especially if anyone was really liquored up. Remember, we were still two or three years away from 21. Drinking was not only illegal; it was against the school code of conduct. So anyone who was weaving, unable to stand up, or passed out still had to somehow make the trip past Father O'Leary's door without him knowing. We discovered that if one guy asked to go to confession with Father Tim, he would close his door. That left the rest of us free to tiptoe past while carrying our friend.

Years later a group of us former students met for a reunion. We dearly loved Father O'Leary, so we made sure he would also be able to come. At dinner, he started telling stories from the old days.

"I always thought it was pretty funny when you guys would send someone to confession so you could bring in a drunken kid or something like that. I was delighted to let some drunk go by without me having to get involved *and* I got a kid for confession that I could talk to for a while." He knew everything! He really wasn't that grim after all.

Father O'Leary was a great mentor for me. I enjoyed his organic chemistry class. He was also the person who steered me toward Creighton University School of Medicine. And one other memory of my shenanigans involves him. In my sophomore year (1960), John F. Kennedy was running for president against Richard Nixon. My friends and I just loved Kennedy. We loved his ideas, his youth, his Catholicism... JFK inspired us. So, the banner with Nixon and his running mate's names strung across Riverside Avenue in Spokane irritated us no end. Every time I drove my '49 Ford (The Loganberry

Lady) down that street, Nixon/Lodge flapped happily in the breeze. To my 18-year-old self, the banner's existence felt like a taunt.

We decided that the least we could do to help the cause was to take the banner down. Two guys went to the far side of the street, climbed a fence, scaled the fire escape, and waited for us to find our way to the other side, which wasn't as simple. My friend and I had to walk through a meeting room full of union members in the middle of a discussion. We just walked through and said, "Hi, hi," and went right out the window to the fire escape. The guys on the other side cut the rope, and we reeled it in.

We planned to drop the banner down two floors to the pavement and then put it in my car, which was parked around the corner. Easy-peasy, right? No. It was not easy. What we didn't realize until we were holding it was the banner was made of canvas. It weighed hundreds of pounds. We managed to reel it onto the fire escape and then, just as we dropped it to the street below, we realized, "Oh! We could kill someone with this!" We didn't. Thank goodness. The other thing we didn't consider was that Nixon's Republican headquarters was in a street-level office directly under the banner. When the thing came crashing down, a guy stepped out the front door and started yelling at us.

"Hey! You kids! You can't do that!"

We said, "It's ripped! We have to fix it. We're taking it down to fix it!" And maybe three minutes after that, the police arrived.

The union guys whose meeting we interrupted were not impressed. They were afraid our prank would be associated with them and told the police, "We have nothing to do with these boys." The cops put us in their car and started driving to the station. That's when they noticed the Loganberry Lady, which was parked around the corner with no license plates on it for obvious reasons. I was holding my breath, hoping they wouldn't connect us with the sedan. The cop says, "Is that your car, son?" Before I knew it, my car was impounded.

At the police station, they called the university and released us to school officials. We were all worried that charges would be brought against us, but the police decided this was a matter for Gonzaga to handle. So we only had to worry about getting expelled instead of charged with a crime. Not much better, really.

My buddies and I had to go before a committee to explain ourselves. I remember we encouraged each other beforehand. We swore we were going to stand up for our values. We were Kennedy people, and our actions were noble—righteous even! That whole notion dissolved when we entered the conference room and discovered a forbidding line of black-frocked priests all frowning at us and shaking their heads. It was all over. In that moment, we saw ourselves through their eyes. We were just foolish boys who had made a mess of things.

They said, "This type of thing is not acceptable. You just can't do that, and you especially cannot do so when a Catholic is running for president and you attend a Catholic university!" We had publicly embarrassed the priests and the university. We had made it seem like the Catholics were out to sabotage Nixon. I kept waiting to hear the word "expelled." Instead, our punishment was service. We had to set up chairs for all the Gonzaga meetings, forever—or it seemed like forever. It was probably a semester or so. Every week or so, a group of us would show up in the evening to set up dozens of folding chairs. And then come back at the end and take them all down. Every time, some elderly woman would rave over us, saying how wonderful we boys were. So kind to set up all the chairs! The priests never told why we were really there.

The funniest part of the entire hubbub was Father O'Leary's reaction. He sat on the committee of priests who gave us hell. But a few weeks afterwards, he called me into his office. He looked at me and said, "How'd you do that? How'd you get that banner down? Did you have to send kids up the fire escape...?" He disapproved, but his inner teenager wanted to know exactly how we pulled it off. See what I mean? He really wasn't grim at all.

Father O'Leary was a wise man and he was also a man of great faith. Years later, when he was very ill, he told one of my friends that he couldn't understand what all the fuss about dying was about. "It's just like walking from one room to another."

I continued to be very enthusiastic for John Kennedy. He was young, handsome, and dynamic. He cared about the poor; he was a Democrat, and, of course, Catholic—the first Catholic nominated for president since Al Smith's crushing defeat to Herbert Hoover in 1928. I already knew who Kennedy was. I had closely watched the Democratic convention in 1956, when Kennedy barely lost to Estes Kefauver for the vice-presidential nomination. Losing that opportunity was probably good for Kennedy, since Stevenson/Kefauver lost badly to Eisenhower/Nixon, running for their second term.

By 1960, Kennedy was well known nationally, though he still had a problem with his public perception. People wondered if he was too young, too inexperienced, and maybe too Catholic? My mother told me, "Don't get too excited about Kennedy. Some people, even good people, just can't bring themselves to vote for a Catholic when they get in the voting booth. I lived through Al Smith in 1928. It will probably be the same with Kennedy."

Well, I was still excited. When JFK came to speak at Gonzaga, I was genuinely thrilled. I recall being surprised that he had an accent, a fairly pronounced Massachusetts accent. I guess I had never heard him speak before. And he also had humor. I recall one line from his speech: "If we do not control nuclear bombs, mankind will face the danger of destroying a quarter of the world's population in one fell swoop, a feat not accomplished since Cain slew Abel." I loved that line.

After his talk, we gathered on Division Street and walked to the convention center where the Washington state Democratic Convention was being held. Kennedy was in an open convertible and I was able to walk right next to the car, just a few feet from him. When we got to the convention center, the future president stood up in the car and said we were not allowed in the center, but he pointed at some doors and said, why don't you go over there and wait. A few minutes later, the doors flew open and half a dozen guys ran out, yelling, "Come in, come in, come in!" We went in and marched around the auditorium, chanting "JFK! JFK! JFK!" The Democratic convention folks were actually quite pleasant. The organist joined in leading the JFK chant, and we were led around the seating area and onto the stage. There, as we paraded across, all the Democratic Party candidates who were there met us, smiled and shook our hands as we were happily led out the door, back to the street. It was fun and no one seemed upset about it.

I remained a very enthusiastic supporter for John Kennedy until the day he was assassinated in Dallas (November 22, 1963). That day, I was a sophomore medical student at Creighton. At lunchtime, we learned that he had been shot but we went ahead with class. At the end of class, we were told he had died. A classmate standing next to me said, "Serves the son-of-a-bitch right." At our Class of 1966 50th year medical school class reunion, I sat next to that guy at dinner. I did not mention his remark, but I remembered.

I previously mentioned the "Loganberry Lady," my car that the police had impounded when we got caught taking the Nixon-Lodge banner over Riverside Avenue down. That was a car that I had bought on the Yakama reservation for $100. It was a 1949 Ford, Loganberry red (I was told), lowered, with "pipes" and no front grill. I had to drive very slowly across railroad tracks or it would hit bottom.

Somehow, I lost the keys or something so I had to hot-wire it every time I started it. I never got new keys. I just left the starter wires hanging down under the dashboard in the car, which was always unlocked. Anyone could get in it, hot-wire it, and drive it off. It just sat in front of my house at home or on the campus in Spokane. I thought it was great, slowly bouncing down the road, but one day when I was driving from Spokane to Toppenish in a rainstorm it just quit on the highway, near Sprague, Washington. I left it by the side of the road and hitchhiked home. I called the state patrol and asked them to have it towed somewhere, anywhere. When I called the junkyard in Sprague where it had been towed, they said I owed more money than the car was worth, but a high school kid there would give me $50 for the car and pay the storage fee. I said okay. A month later, when I hadn't received any money, I went to Sprague High School, found the student, and demanded the money. He said the car was still in the junkyard. The block was cracked. He said it was worthless and I could have it back. I said no, you're stuck with it and I left. I don't know what happened to the car. Neither the high school kid nor the junkyard man ever called me, and I never went back to check on it.

Sometime later, I was able to buy a beautiful light blue 1955 two-door Chevy Bel Air from our next-door neighbor in Toppenish. He was elderly and hardly ever drove it. The car was in perfect condition, except that it didn't have a radio. He was deaf and didn't think he needed one when he bought it. It lasted until I was well out of medical school. The last couple of years that I owned the Chevy, the reverse gear didn't work. You had to be careful where you parked your car when you didn't have a reverse. Incidentally, for a long time, I wondered why people referred to my beautiful light blue car as aqua. I guess it really was aqua color, but it looked blue to me and I loved it.

IV – Summer Jobs

This segue between shenanigans and summer jobs seems like a good time to tell the story about the time I got arrested. (Not to be confused with the time I got taken in for the banner incident, but then let go.)

Every summer, I found whatever work I could get. I still had a strong relationship with Safeway in Toppenish, so I would put in shifts there in summer and on holiday breaks. And because the staff all knew me, they would save merchandise for me to put out. I remember coming in to work at the end of the day and there would be many carts waiting to be stocked on the shelves. So, the store would close, I would crank up the radio and grab a mop and work until morning. I enjoyed those times.

On nights when I wasn't working, I liked to go out with friends. Sometimes we would drink beer. On this particular night we had barely finished high school. I think I was 17 or 18 years old. That night, my buddies and I decided we wanted more beer. The Tampico Tavern was still open, so we headed there, knowing we needed to be careful. The Tampico was immediately adjacent to the police station. (You can see where this is going, can't you?)

My buddies talked me into stepping out of the car to find a buyer for us. So, I waited until a friendly-looking guy came out of the bar. He was young, black, and approachable. I figured he would remember what it was like to be me. So I walked up to him and said, "Hey, man, would you buy me a couple of jugs of beer?" "Sure," he said and went back inside. When he came out with the two jugs, I gave him the money, looped my fingers through the handles and turned around to head to the car. That's when I saw the police car. It was slowly pulling up to the curb right in front of me and the cops inside seemed to be waiting to see what I would do. Well, what else could I do? I put the jugs right on the ground and started walking away. The black kid started walking the other way.

"Hey, son!" I sighed and faced the policeman again. One of the cops had gotten out of his car to talk to me, and over his shoulder I noticed my buddy's 1949 Mercury easing away from the curb and idling down the block with my five so-called friends inside. I was stranded with no backup. "Get in the car," he said.

When I got in the front seat between the policemen, I sat on a billy club. I reached down, pulled up the club to hand it to them. And both of them go, "Holy Jesus!" and ducked, covering their heads until they figured out that I was just trying to give the billy club to them. When they hauled me into the police station, they said, "We don't care about you drinking, we just want to get that nigger."

"What do you have against black people?"

"Oh God, one of them!" The cop rolled his eyes at me.

The cops figured out quickly that I wasn't going to be much help to them. They threatened to put me in jail right then, but decided instead to send me home with my mother. Except when I called her, she said, "I can't come and get you." The officers were clearly done with me for the night, so they let me go. I walked home with the stipulation that I show up for a court hearing on the matter in two days.

On the appointed day, I arranged to take my lunch hour from Safeway to clear up the mess. I tried to stop off at the law office of a family friend, but of course he was gone. So, I walked into court alone, and everybody looked at me like I was crazy. I sat down at the defendant table feeling very uneasy. The judge and everyone came in, and then the cop who arrested me arrived with my two jugs of beer, which he placed on the table, and he sat down in the witness chair. I gathered that the jugs of beer were Exhibit A.

"How do you plead?"

I said, "I plead guilty."

He said, "Do you have anything you wish to say to the court?"

I said, "No."

The policeman stood up, picked up the two jugs of beer and left the courtroom. And everyone in the court just looked at each other. I got the feeling that I could have handled this entire episode better. Maybe I should have made sure I had a lawyer to help me, but I figured that out too late. Later, I learned that I had the option of just paying a $25 fine and skipping the entire court appearance.

The judge said to me, "Well, you pled guilty. You had your chance to say something. I'll give you something you will remember—twenty-four hours in jail starting now."

I had no choice then but to do what I was told. I left the courtroom and walked around the corner to the booking counter at the jail. Sitting at the counter was an officer. He lived two blocks from our house and knew me pretty well. Without looking up he said, "Put your stuff on the counter... Joe! What are you doing here?!"

I said, "Well, I had this problem with some beer, but I've got to go back to work so I would like to serve this twenty-four hours another day, maybe?"

He frowned at me and said, "No. You can't. You should have told that to the judge but it is too late now." He was surprised at my situation, but he still had a job to do. "You've got one phone call, and you are going to jail."

So I called up George Long and said, "Tell my boss I am not going back to work this afternoon because I am in jail. Call my mother and tell her I won't be home tonight because I am in jail. And bring a clean pair of clothes to work tomorrow because I'll be out by noon, and I'll come straight back to work after that."

George said, "Uh...okay, Joe. Will do."

Jail is interesting. Capacity in the Toppenish jail was about 40, but there were more like 60 men in there that day. Each cell contained two double beds, four men to a cell. Except there were six guys in the cell with me. Most of the other inmates were brown-skinned guys. Lots of Mexicans. Many Indians, even though Indians weren't supposed to be there at all. Tribal law is independent of the county and the Yakama nation has their own police and court system. All afternoon and evening the cops brought more people in. Many of them were drunk and singing loudly and generally raising hell, until they saw me standing there, a Caucasian, clean-cut kid in a white work shirt. "What the hell are you doing here?" they would ask.

There were so many guys in the cell with me, I had to sleep on the floor with my head next to the toilet. Sometime during the night, somebody got picked up and he gave me his blanket on the way out. I remember being a little intimidated by all these rough-looking men at first, but they were nice. They all wrote me notes to give to their friends when I got out.

The next day at noon, I was free. I ran to the Safeway, got changed into the clean clothes from George, and took my check stand like the last 24 hours had never happened. It was definitely weird to go from the dirty jail floor to the bright clean store without even pausing in between to stop and think things over. My manager came over and said, "Nice to see you, Joe." I began to think maybe this whole ordeal would blow over quickly. He was nice to me; maybe others would be too.

Then I saw my first customer for the day. It was a beautiful girl from church that I had a crush on. She was perfect, and I would have loved to have a date with her. Behind the girl was her mother, whose wide grin showed she had no intention of letting my indiscretion go. "I hear you had an interesting evening, Joe." Ugh. I turned red. Then I jammed the whole cash register. The drawer wouldn't open, and they stood there watching me struggling and embarrassed. I thought, *My life is ruined.*

My mother was appalled. She said, "I am a schoolteacher! Don't you know the police love to get the schoolteachers' kids?! And don't you *ever* tell Pat or anyone back in the Midwest!"

And my buddies? They still tease me about my time in the slammer… and I can still see them driving off while I am being arrested.

I don't want to give the impression that all I did was mess around as a young man. The stories of getting in trouble stick out in my memory *because* they were outside the norm. Most of the time, I was trying hard to be a good kid and make a little money to pay for school. My mother's teaching salary went only so far. I wasn't deeply involved in how much school cost. I counted on my mom to pay the bills, but I gave her my paychecks to help out as much as possible.

Starting the summer between my freshman and sophomore years at Gonzaga, I worked for a trucking outfit owned by a friend's father. Dennis Richardson had been a good friend through high school and a roommate at college. His father, Norman Richardson, owned a trucking business that contracted with Washington canneries to bring the harvested peas and corn in from the fields every summer. Since it paid much more than Safeway, I was grateful for the job.

My responsibility in this operation was to drive a tractor that had been converted into a forklift. It's a little convoluted to describe in print, but the conversion becomes important in this story, so I'll take the time to explain how it worked. To make a tractor into a tractor/forklift, a forklift was attached to the back of the tractor, which I used to lift metal bins full of peas onto the transport trucks. To balance the enormous loads of peas, they placed a huge concrete block on the front end of the tractor by the engine. Then they rotated the driver's seat 180 degrees, so I sat backwards to better keep an eye on the fork lifting the bins of peas to move them to the truck. That meant that when I drove, I kind of scooted around in the seat so I could keep one hand on the steering wheel and one eye on my payload.

In the field, the pea vines were put into large machines that spat the peas into a large bin at the bottom. Next, I picked up the bin with the forklift and put it on the truck. Back and forth I drove from the harvester to the truck, harvester to truck, up and down the rows of the pea field for 12 hours a day. It was quite an operation. As soon as my shift was done, another guy would come take my place and work the next shift. The work continued nonstop, 24 hours a day.

After a month working outdoors every day, I felt like I was finally getting a suntan. With my Irish complexion, I had never really been able to get that brown skin other people could. I was motoring along, enjoying my new look, when Mr. Richardson stopped me in my tracks.

"What the hell is the matter with you, Lynch? Are you sick?"

"No," I said.

"Are you working days?"

"Yeah." I looked down at my arms and noticed how inflamed they actually looked.

"You are on nights from now on."

I was crusty with sunburns and didn't realize that it probably was not good for me until I saw the look on his face. But nights were okay too. They kept big, open vats of coffee steaming out there for the workers. Between the soil, the coffee, the diesel, the peas...it smelled heavenly out there. I just loved it. We worked away through the day and night, our harvesting equipment nibbling its way through the field of peas that seemed as big as an ocean. When we finally got to the end, there would be the corn waiting for us, almost ripe enough for harvest. It usually needed another couple of weeks to reach maturity, so we got a short break after the peas were done.

When I wasn't at work, I was sleeping at a motel in Walla Walla with the rest of the crew. The only days we got off were the rainy ones. It was always nice to have a little break once in a while, but we got paid by the hour, so the more hours I worked, the better. Some of the guys went out at night, but it was all I could do to work, eat, shower and sleep, and then repeat it the next day and the next day and the next day. I was grateful to Dennis for getting me the job and to his father, Norman Richardson, for employing a kid who knew nothing about farming or trucking. He was patient with me, probably more patient than he should have been.

During those down weeks most other kids got laid off, but Mr. Richardson seemed committed to keeping me working. He knew I was trying to pay for college expenses and probably felt some kindness in his heart for his son's childhood friend. He gave the order to his foreman to "keep Lynch working." I remember meeting with the head mechanic to find me some work to do.

He asked, "Do you know anything about working on the truck engines?"

"No."

"Do you know how to change the oil on the trucks?"

"No."

He paused, and said, "Well, do you know how to make coffee?"

I said, "No." I ended up washing trucks for a couple of weeks.

I was really testing the level of commitment Mr. Richardson had for me, but that wasn't the worst thing that happened. That first summer I was driving the forklift, really in the groove going back and forth. Zoom to the pea harvester, scoop up the bin, put the tractor in reverse, back up, turn, and put the peas on the truck. Reverse the whole thing. Repeat. Over and over for 12 hours every day I did that. I got so I didn't really have to think hard about what I was doing and could look up at the stars or the clouds, depending on the time of day. One time, I picked up the bin, got the tractor rolling and *then* looked over my shoulder—oh no! As I swung the rig around, Norman Richardson's Cadillac was right behind me. When did that get there?!

When you're in an accident, your brain captures every single moment in detail, so I can still see in slow motion how I stomped on the brake; the tractor wheels stopped moving, but the vehicle did not. There in front of God and everybody, the whole rig skidded across the dirt, pulled forward by the weight of that two-ton concrete block. Millisecond by millisecond, the rig continued forward until it came to rest against my boss's shiny white Cadillac. Crrrrunch. The awful noise of that block caving in the driver-side door of my boss's car matched the sound of my crumpling pride.

The field was deadly silent. Everyone was waiting to see what would happen next. I looked up and saw Norman Richardson, maybe ten yards away, observing the whole episode. He just calmly walked over, opened the passenger-side door of his damaged car, slid awkwardly across the front seat and drove away.

I thought for sure I would be fired. Anybody else causing that kind of damage on a worksite would be. But once again, I got lucky. I wasn't fired. Despite the hoots and hollers from the guys who saw what happened ("Look where you're going, Lynch!"), I heard nothing about it from management. I finally asked Dennis, "What'd your dad say?" Dennis reported his Dad's reaction: "I should have never parked there, period." And that was the end of the discussion.

Every June, July, and August between 1959 and 1962, I returned to work the peas and corn. It was demanding, but lucrative. And I learned a lot on this job, both about the value of hard work and about the life of a laborer. After a year or two on the tractor, they let me drive trucks. Mr. Richardson had purchased a bunch of wonderful old Diamond T trucks. These are the rounded fender, World War

II-era trucks you might see in a parade. Even in 1960, the fleet was so worn out that I could see the road below me through holes in the flooring. I remember one night I hit a bump on the farm road and the headlights went out. I had to drive blind until I hit another bump that turned them back on.

The trucks never really stopped during the summer. They made a three- or four-hour run to the fields, got loaded, and headed back to Libby's Cannery in Walla Walla. Then back to the field. Then back to the cannery until the shift was done. At the beginning of every shift, there was a row of eight or ten drivers in the field office waiting to get called. You didn't earn money unless you were driving. And if I was sitting there, even at the back of the line, the dispatcher would call me, "Lynch, you're up."

I went over, replaced the day driver, and I was set for 10, 12, or 14 hours. If nobody called your name and all the trucks had come and gone they said, "See you in twelve hours. You'll take the next shift." While sitting there, I talked to those guys. They were all nice and they all treated me fine, despite the favoritism. I realized these guys had kids. They had homes and families to support, and here I was, an inexperienced kid taking hours that would have been theirs. I knew that they were better than me at driving those trucks, and I knew that they weren't making much money. That realization made me want to go to college because I would never be as handy as they were.

That experience taught me that there are a lot of jobs in the world where people are working pretty hard, and they are not getting paid much. There's nothing wrong with labor. I admired those guys for their skill at driving and their ability to fix the trucks as they broke down. But I could see the world isn't equal. Some jobs pay more than others. Also, if I was expected to compete with them—say I continued this line of work—there would come a day when I would be demoted. They were better than I was at driving, and this favoritism from the boss was a limited-time offer. It made me want to study hard in college.

V – Pre-Med in Three Years

Back at Gonzaga, I continued to take courses in pre-med. My advisor, Father O'Leary, encouraged me to apply to Creighton University and see if I could get accepted after only three years at Gonzaga. This was a long shot. Most students needed four years of pre-med study to be accepted to their school of medicine. But he said I should try anyway. "Once in a while they will take a good student after only three years."

I applied to Creighton that fall. They accepted me in January, and my mother, my sister and I began wondering how to pay for it. I suspect Father O'Leary had something to do with my acceptance. A nudge from the chairman of the chemistry department works wonders. Plus the doctor that had delivered me wrote me a recommendation. This was Dr. L.J. DeBacker, my brother-in-law's father. Creighton was his alma mater and perhaps that helped too.

I remember thinking that maybe I could be a doctor. I had role models in my life that I admired and thought of as doing well financially. (Though, in retrospect, a physician practicing in Toppenish can't really have been that well off.) I probably couldn't conceive of what it would mean to care for patients at age 20. But I was doing pretty well in my classes, and the structure of med school appealed to me. I had some misgivings but I didn't know what else I could do for a living. So, off to Creighton I went.

Chapter 5

Creighton Years, 1962-1966

I – I Guess I'll Be a Doctor

There are some people who grow up knowing exactly what they want to be when they grow up. Many, like me, do not have that vision. We float around a little bit, trying one set of clothes on, and then another, until we find a set that seems to fit. As a young man, the uncertainty of not knowing my career path caused me some discomfort. I didn't know what I wanted; I only knew there were many things I absolutely did not want to do for a living. I felt a responsibility to make my mother proud. And to find a vocation that would make enough money that she wouldn't need to worry about me anymore.

I was a little surprised to find myself at medical school. I hadn't aimed that high in life, but I was pretty good at the classes and I enjoyed the material. I probably didn't know at age 20, but looking back now I can say that medicine was exactly the right field for me. Plus, to be honest, it really is a lot easier to finish a graduate degree where there is assigned course work (like a medical degree has) versus picking a specialty and writing a Ph.D. dissertation. I think it's safe to say that I thrive in structured environments. Once I really got going at Creighton Medical School, that's exactly what happened.

During some of our country's most turbulent years, 1962 through 1966, I was studying at Creighton University School of Medicine. We had the Cuban missile crisis, the assassination of a president, the war in Vietnam, and what looked like a war for civil rights throughout much of America. Then, in 1968, Martin Luther King and Robert Kennedy were assassinated, two months apart. The sixties were a violent time. Some of that turbulence spilled into my life. For the most part, I was paying attention to my studies, trying to figure out how to be a grown-up (of sorts), and getting out for some occasional fun. Becoming a doctor is a lot of work. Medical school was four years long, followed by six more years of specialty and subspecialty training. Including my undergraduate years at Gonzaga, it took me 13 years of post-high school education before I would be able to practice medicine.

As I've said, I didn't really know where I was going when I started. I think that approach—seeing what seems to fit my skills and then choosing more of that kind of thing—has served me well. For instance, Human Anatomy lab pointed me in a direction. We didn't know then, but our cadaver team of five future doctors jumped into the roles we would ultimately be in for the rest of our lives. There were two guys on my team who could not wait to touch the cadaver and get in there with scalpels. I almost never touched that body. I didn't find it nearly as fascinating as reading through the book to find out how the processes worked. I wanted to understand what was happening. I didn't feel the need to be the one with the instrument. The two who *did* have that burning desire became surgeons. As a designated "reader" of our group, I became an internist: the one who figures out what's wrong and refers people to those surgeons.

Though anatomy was an interesting diversion, the rest of my classes that first semester nearly killed me. At Creighton, they ran something called the core system, which at the time was thought to be very innovative. Medical students took only biochemistry classes for the first six weeks. I wasn't very good at it, I didn't particularly like the chairman, and I felt myself falling behind. At the end of those six weeks, a third of the students got called in, including me. They said, "You're not cutting it, you're never going to graduate."

That was very frightening. I thought, *I can't be a doctor. I'm no good at this.*

Over a weekend, I went to visit my sister in Grand Island. There at the house was a family friend, an older doctor. He asked, "How you doing in school, Joe?"

"Not very good," I said. "I'm not sure I'm gonna pass biochemistry. And if I can't pass how am I ever gonna be a doctor?"

His response has stuck with me forever. He said, "Biochemistry, you can't let something like that stop you from being a doctor. It's really got nothing to do with practicing medicine."

And I thought, "Oh! It's just a hurdle. I get it. It's a hurdle." I'd had classes like that before. Organic chemistry at Gonzaga was a hurdle too, and I had passed that class. I could see then that my biochemistry professor didn't have the power to say whether I could or could not be a doctor. He was just a barrier I needed to clear so I could get to the next step. I passed the class and things were okay.

II – Paying for Med School

You might be wondering how a single mother/teacher could afford to send her son to medical school. I'm a little ashamed to say that I did not wonder about that. At least not until the Yakima County sheriff went to arrest my mother for tax fraud.

When my blue-haired, 4' 10" mother was confronted by the sheriff on her front porch, she was understandably frightened. He explained that the IRS had been in touch with him, that her income taxes were completely messed up, and had been for some time. She was not allowed to claim a 23-year-old as a dependent.

And that's where my mother had a foothold in the argument. She explained many things: that she didn't know her taxes were wrong, that she would try to do better, and that her 23-year-old son absolutely *was* a dependent. Though the sheriff had intended to arrest her that day, after looking at her and hearing her argument he said, "Well, okay. Let me work on this."

The final solution he worked out stipulated that Cecilia Lynch (my mom) hire an accountant and sort things out with the IRS. Mom said that accountant was the best investment she ever made. "He made money for me every year."

I tried to help from my end too. I wrote a letter to the IRS in Seattle, firmly pointing out that if they spent more time trying to convict Jimmy Hoffa (who was free at that time) and less time attacking 4' 10" blue-haired, second-grade schoolteachers, this would be a better country. I was kind of proud of that letter.

The IRS wrote me back. They wanted more information. So my mother and I detailed our financial arrangement for them. We explained about my job working the pea harvest. We shared my process of signing over those paychecks directly to her for deposit in her bank. During the school year she paid the tuition, food, and housing bills. Once a month, I sent her a list of all my expenses to help her keep track. Mom eventually got a response from the IRS. They said any 23-year-old—boy or man—who sent a monthly summary of his expenses to his mother is a dependent. And that is how the IRS declared that I was, indeed, a momma's boy.

Honestly, that didn't bother me. It was pretty evident to anyone who knew me that I was dependent on her. I knew I was working day and night, as hard as I could, and I was okay with accepting help from my mother.

During my junior year in med school, Mom finally asked me to take out some loans for the remainder of my education so she could retire. She had been teaching well past the mandatory retirement age in Washington (65 years old). She told me every year the Superintendent of Schools would walk past her in the halls and say, "Cecilia, I could have sworn you were 65." Finally one year he pulled her into his office and said he was sorry, but it was time to stop teaching.

I agreed to take over financial responsibility for my education. I still marvel at the fact that my mom—the woman who was once so helpless her family despaired for her future—not only thrived while raising her child alone, but sent him to six years of college without debt!

III – Accidental Hijinks

Major exams were usually on Mondays and we would study almost around the clock through the preceding weekend. Sometimes, some of us would go to Sunday 4:00 a.m. mass at St. John's. There was always an interesting group attending mass at that time, the night people of Omaha: policemen, milkmen, hospital workers, and an occasional vagrant. I always enjoyed the people-watching. I had to study very hard in med school, sometimes all night long. To stay awake and to help the information settle in, I would occasionally leave my desk and go for a walk in the middle of the night. In my sophomore year at Creighton, that habit got me in trouble with the police (again), though this time I was completely innocent.

While out for a very long walk, I was stopped by police around 2:00 a.m. They were looking for a suspect that matched my description. Someone who looked like me and wore similar clothing had just attempted to rape a nursing student. I was shocked and saddened to hear that. But I had been wandering around in the dark for a long time. I had no witnesses to prove it wasn't me. They took me into the station for questioning, and grew more and more suspicious and aggressive as they matched up the evidence in the case with details that happened to line up with me. My status as a medical student added to their case, because that gave me opportunity to know the poor girl.

I knew the area well, having lived and worked nearby for a couple years by then. It was also near where I had spent my summers with my sister Pat and her family. I had an awful time explaining myself and was getting scared. I didn't have a reason for being out that night; I was just talking a walk!

After hours of questioning and waiting, the police had me call six or seven roommates down to the station so they could fill in a lineup. The first time I called, they hung up, thinking it was a prank call. I had to call back and quickly say, "Don't hang up, don't hang up, this is serious." The two detectives quizzing me suddenly got nicer when they heard my friends pull up outside the police station, laughing and joking about the whole thing. The guys thought the situation was hilarious and smiled and teased through the process, but they also vouched for my character. "No way could Joe be the guy you're looking for." But I was worried.

When the young woman looked at us in the lineup, I realized it would not be hard to pick me out, as I was the only one without a grin on my face. I thought, *What if she thinks I look like the guy?* Soon afterward, the girl smiled and even laughed a little bit at us and indicated that I wasn't the person who had attacked her. Thankfully, the police let me go. The episode taught me that sometimes the so-called facts can come together in a way that can make an innocent person look guilty. I also realized that the detectives actually were hoping that I was guilty. It was nothing personal, but if I was the guilty person, then that would solve the case and they could go on to something else. Besides, I was their only suspect. The episode did make me a bit of a celebrity at school for a time.

IV – Service in the Amazon

The only summer vacation medical students get is after their first year. I was glad for the break after that academic obstacle course. I used some of the time to visit my sister, Pat, in Grand Island. During the visit, I met an extraordinary man who would influence my faith and my future career, Father Constance Krupski. When I asked, "What do you do for a living?" he replied, "Well, I work in the Amazon. Every four years I get to come up to the United States for six months to raise funds for my work there."

I said, "The Amazon, really, that's fascinating."

Father Krupski said, "Everybody says that and nobody visits."

"I'll visit you," I said.

I was mostly being polite, but that promise stuck with me like burrs in my socks. Father Krupski explained that he had built a mission in Almeirim, Brazil. But his project wasn't your standard "handouts and Bibles" type of charity. He was working on creating a brick factory so local citizens could earn their own money and raise their standard of living. He pestered and begged doctors to come provide health care for the medical post he had established. He even built a community soccer field with volunteer help. In all these kindnesses, Father Krupski won the love of that community. He understood that no one really wants charity. They want resources so they can raise their own standard of living.

I was fascinated by the exotic man in my sister's living room. I wanted to go see his mission in Brazil. It seemed fun, and I admired this man who spent so much time and effort in service to others. I had to borrow money to make the trip happen. Doing so seemed a little frivolous at the time, since my medical education was already so expensive. My mom was hoping I would work all that summer since there would be no more long breaks after this year. But I consulted with a classmate who already had a wife and several children. "Oh God, go!" he said. "You'll never be able to do something like this after you get married and have kids. Do it now."

I tried to line up some traveling companions. Two other classmates indicated that they would come, but when the day came to fly out, I was at the airport and they were not. I made my way to the port town of Belém, at the mouth of the Amazon. Then I took a very rough plane ride up the Amazon to Santarem, and then caught a boat ride with some Franciscans going my direction. I got off in Almeirim and was greeted with open arms by Father Krupski.

I was 21, on my own along the Amazon River with an old family friend, and a bunch of villagers. I thought that was the height of adventure. And it was. I remember following Father around, trying to learn Portuguese. He wanted me to use my medical education to benefit the villagers, who were all very poor. I tried to explain that I still hadn't had any clinical training; the first two years of med school are all in the classroom. But before we were finished with the discussion, someone pounded on his door.

"We have a problem with a baby being delivered, will you come?"

What else could I do but go try to help? The hut I entered was creepy. Dark and smoky, it smelled like sweat, and blood, and fear. There were women in the village that had much more knowledge of childbirth than I did, but no one had ever seen a delivery like this one. The mother was carrying quintuplets. After one would emerge, another would take its place. It just seemed to go on and on. It was like nothing anyone had ever seen. Two of those babies survived, three died, and the mother died. To survive, they would have needed care and the kind of equipment that hadn't yet been invented and certainly wasn't available in a rural Brazilian village. Father Krupski had given the family money to go to Belém for medical care, but they did not use it for that. Understandably, he was upset.

That was the most dramatic event of my time in the Amazon. Visiting such a different place at that age and stage in my education was eye opening. It helped me see how fortunate people in the United

States are, and how life altering it can be to have simple things like clean water and knowledge of hygiene and health.

I could see how Father's vision of a medical clinic could make a huge difference, and I wanted to be the guy to make it happen. I would have stayed with Father Krupski another year if not for a slow-moving postal service. In order to stay, I needed a leave of absence from school. I sent that request to Creighton; however, by mid-August I hadn't heard back. My heart wanted to stay, but my brain said, "Don't get yourself thrown out of school." So, I headed back to Nebraska for the start of the academic year. When I walked into the medical school the Associate Dean seemed flummoxed. "What the hell are you doing here!? I thought you were taking a year in the Amazon?" They had approved my leave of absence, but I didn't receive it in time. By then it was too late to go back. So I settled in for another year of studying.

V – Meeting Martzie

For my sophomore year, I lived in a duplex near the Phi Rho Sigma house where I had been living as a freshman. I'm not psychologically a "frat guy," but Creighton didn't have student housing for medical students. Living at "Rho House" solved many problems: housing, food, friends...old exams. It worked out well.

Sometime that year, a Gonzaga friend contacted me while visiting Omaha. Charles Braunger and I had been roommates in Spokane. He was there visiting his sister Mary Ellen, who was enrolled in medical technology school at Creighton. I think he thought I might like his sister and probably wanted her to meet a few people on campus. While showing them around the fraternity, I learned that Mary Ellen preferred to be called Martzie, and that she liked music. I liked her. I thought she was pretty, and eventually asked her out. We dated off and on for my remaining years at Creighton.

Martzie and I enjoyed dancing at the basement fraternity parties. On Fridays, the fraternity would hire maybe three guys from north Omaha to play the tunes of the day: Little Richard, Trini Lopez, and the Beatles. (Though, to be honest, I always thought the Beatles were a little tinny. Never really liked them.) Phi Rho Sigma had converted a Dr. Pepper machine into a "beer machine," which meant there was always a cold supply of Falstaff available for 25 cents. During parties they also sold drinks at the bar down there, which funded the next party. All of this was totally illegal, though no one ever said anything. I remember dancing and drinking with Martzie until midnight, when the band would quit and say they were going home. We would demand more money from the fraternity treasurer, who always said no. So, we passed the hat to get the band to stay a little longer.

Dating Martzie was fun and sometimes frustrating. We would get along, and then break up. Then reunite again and repeat the cycle. I remember feeling like this was the time in my life I should be finding a wife. I was 22, had figured out a career path. The next step in life was starting a family. Martzie was from a Catholic family in Sioux City that was much like my sister Pat's family. Twelve kids, devotion to church and family, it all seemed like a good match. We were on track to get married and that seemed like the right path to be on at the time.

VI – Finishing Medical School

In 1965, I finally got to touch patients. I was a junior in medical school, working at Douglas County Hospital under resident supervisors. The attending physician in charge of the entire ward was a man I would come to respect and appreciate, though when we first met, I was scared of Dr. Andy Hahn. He was a no-nonsense kind of guy who would get quite annoyed at residents if they or their medical students got something wrong.

In those years, there was no such thing as Medicare. Indigent patients didn't have primary care doctors. So, their conditions often went untreated until they became emergencies, which was when we met them at the hospital. There were many days when patients were lined up in the hallways on gurneys waiting to see a doctor.

Dr. Hahn was in charge of morning report. He figured out that the best way to keep track of all these patients was to review all the x-rays from the previous day. That way "nothing big got by him." Every morning at 7:00 a.m. we were required to attend a meeting. We really liked him, but he was intense and gruff and sometimes seemed fierce. To prepare for Dr. Hahn, the residents would first meet with the medical students at 6:00 a.m. to review all the x-rays. Our job as students was to present the cases to the group and Dr. Hahn. We would describe the x-rays and what we thought was the diagnosis and treatment plan. If we messed up, Dr. Hahn would wheel around and go after our resident, not us med students, because it was the residents' job to make sure we knew what we were talking about.

I recall one morning during a student presentation, the guy said, "And here we have a button showing on the x-ray." Dr. Hahn yelled emphatically, "It's a snap, not a button! A snap is a snap, a button is a button!" *Okay,* I thought. *He wants precision. Duly noted.*

One morning, we were all there, coffee in hand sitting in metal folding chairs, reviewing the previous day's cases. Dr. Hahn, who was very tall, would always rock on his chair's back legs. This particular morning, he tipped just a bit too far. The chair and the doctor fell over backwards with a big crash! The chairs around him all went flying cattywumpus. The dozen students and residents were shocked but knew better than to make a peep. Not one person moved or even looked at him. We just stared straight ahead while he got up, straightened his chair, dusted off his clothes, and sat down again. Then we carried on as if nothing had happened.

Sometime during my junior year, Agatha (Aggie) Brennan invited me to lunch with her. She was my cousin. Her mother, Anne, was my mother's older sister. Aggie was older than me and more like a kindly aunt. She had never married. I considered her the "glue" that helped keep the family in touch with each other. At lunch I noticed that she did not eat, saying she was not hungry. As usual, she was kind and had various personal suggestions for me, such as, "Joe, try to keep the dandruff off your glasses." A couple of months later, when I was making rounds with my attending physician at St. Joseph's Hospital, I was very surprised to discover that Aggie was an inpatient there and very ill. She died shortly afterward. She was 45 years old. A few weeks later, her brother, Joe Brennan, who lived in South Omaha, came to see me. He and his family had been very good to me. He gave me $100. He said Aggie wanted me to have it and said to tell me that I really should buy some new clothes. I had to smile. I loved Aggie. I think everyone did.

As a junior, I discovered that I could earn free room, board, and $12.50 per shift if I covered the emergency room at Jennie Edmundson Hospital in Council Bluffs, Iowa, just across the Missouri River, east of Omaha. The hospital owned a house next door specifically for future doctors like me. In return, the med students took turns covering overnight and weekend shifts. What a great deal! I got to move out of the fraternity and still didn't have to pay rent.

Jennie Edmundson is a private hospital, and fewer of the inner-city poor came there compared to the Douglas County Hospital. However, this was the first time I was really on my own treating patients. I was technically a med student, and there were no attending physicians on site. I had to call someone—a hospital doctor or the patient's personal physician—for guidance or approval. But if someone came in all banged up or very sick, it was on me to help them. I remember being scared about the responsibility, and proud of myself too. These days, that arrangement isn't allowed. It's considered too dangerous for the patients.

My senior year of medical school, I found an even cushier moonlighting job. Archbishop Bergan Mercy Hospital in Omaha needed coverage of the obstetrics ward. They provided the same free room and board in trade for being available for overnight and weekend shifts. One other guy and I lived in a room just off the OB floor and alternated nights being on call. That job hardly required me to do anything, since nurses (and the moms) handled all the early labor. If the baby came before the OB doctor did, I would go help. If the labor was prolonged, an OB expert came and took over the case, which was always a relief since those situations can be so dangerous. So, nurses woke me up to catch the occasional baby and let me sleep the rest of the time.

Meanwhile, Jennie Edmundson sold the house we had been living in and changed the pay arrangement for covering the ER overnight to $25 per shift. So, I could live at Bergan Hospital and still take occasional shifts at Jennie Edmundson during my senior year.

If you add up the hours I was going to school or working at the hospital during the day and the hours I was moonlighting at night, you might wonder when I had time to sleep. There were days when I was up for 30 or more straight hours. I figured out that I really just needed five hours of sleep per night to function normally. I was in my mid-twenties and had energy to burn. If I only got three hours, my late afternoons were filled with burning eyes and trying to stay alert. Without any sleep at all, I would be hurting by noon. My head ached, my eyes burned, and my hair itched. I tried not to do that very often. Attending physicians at med school knew that's what we were doing, and understood we needed to be earning money to survive. Their take was, "As long as I can't tell you were moonlighting, it's okay with us." I made sure to shower and shave before the day started, and most of the time I really felt fine.

VII – Graduating & Growing

In May of 1966, I graduated from Creighton University School of Medicine. I was hoping to skip the tediousness of the ceremony. It was guaranteed to be a long, hot day and I just didn't want to go through it. As I mention in the introduction of this book, I realized after talking to Pat that the graduation ceremony wasn't really about me. It was for Mom. This accomplishment happened because she supported and encouraged me. She got me on the right track with the Jesuit high school, arranged rides to school so I could aim a bit higher in life, and paid for all those years of college on a teacher's salary. That day was a culmination of years of hoping, worrying, struggling, and Mom was proud of me. I was glad she got to come celebrate the fruit of her labor and see me become a doctor.

Almost immediately after receiving my diploma, I began my one-year internship at Creighton Memorial St. Joseph's Hospital in Omaha. Officially, I was specializing in internal medicine. This internship is no longer required for doctors, though for me it was enormously important. It enabled me to work longer and more closely with a mentor, James Sullivan. It gave me exposure to a group of high-risk patients who taught me a lot. And it put me squarely in the middle of the Omaha race riots of 1966.

In my medical career, I have witnessed two major advances that completely changed the way we care for people. One was the eradication of smallpox. That cure never touched my area of specialty, but the second—effective medications to treat hypertension—absolutely did. Before about 1970, strokes were much more common. People only went to the doctor when they were sick, not when they felt fine. Those who had hypertension (high blood pressure) may have been aware of it, but there was not much available to treat it effectively anyway. This meant that the patients I saw at Douglas County Hospital and St. Joe's were often seriously ill. Untreated hypertension causes damage to the arteries and all the body's organs, which manifested in my patients as swelling, difficulty breathing, heart attack, stroke, etc.

As an intern trying to treat these patients, it felt like a time of real bonding with the other residents. A patient might come in bleeding, having difficulty breathing, and I would do what I knew how to do. I could stop the bleeding and regulate heart rate, but then I would call a surgery resident upstairs. "This is more than I can handle," I would say. And he would come down and help.

The hospital environment was so friendly and supportive, in large part because of our mentor, Dr. James Sullivan. We called him Sully. He was a really special guy. In charge of Internal Medicine Training, he supervised the residents and interns, and worked at three different hospitals: Douglas County, St. Joe's, and the VA. During one of my first rotations on the wards at the County hospital, Dr. Sullivan told us he would make attending (supervising) rounds with us in the evening. Although I initially thought it was rude of him to have rounds in the evening, I soon found that he was doing us a great favor. There was no one available to make attending rounds so he just said he would do it himself, adding it on to all his other duties. That's why he made rounds in the evenings with us. As always, he did a wonderful job.

When you first saw Sully, you might think him odd. And he was. He walked with a limp from an injury sustained at the Battle of the Bulge. His fingers often twitched, and he smoked a pipe at all times, indoors and outdoors. Sometimes, he would put the lit pipe in his jacket pocket during a meeting. On at least two occasions, smoke started coming out of his pocket; he would take the coat off, step on it to put out the ember, put it back on and carry on with the meeting.

Sully was a friend to interns and residents. We respected him immensely because he made it known he would help us out. One of my friends, a surgery resident named Paul, told me about a time at County when he and the other residents decided to go on strike. They were being asked to do too much and getting next to no money for it, so they opted to walk out rather than cover the emergency room. They notified the administration, whose response was, "Strike if you want, we haven't got any money to pay you more." So the day came for the strike. Paul left the ward, walked through the emergency room going to his car, glanced to his right, and sitting at the desk was Dr. Sullivan.

Paul said, "Hi, Dr. Sullivan."

"Hi, good to see you, Paul."

Paul walked out, got in the car, closed the door and went, "Oh no."

No resident showed up for the emergency room due to the strike, but Sully wasn't going to leave the hospital's patients without care.

Paul put his white coat back on, walked into the ER, and said, "Dr. Sullivan, get out of here." And the strike was broken. Well, it never really got underway. Sully made that happen, not by arguing or negotiating. He just went down and made his presence felt. Everyone loved him so much that they weren't going to let him suffer for their cause.

Sully also made the schedule for the interns. He would call a meeting at his house, provide beer, and sit us down to hash out the plan. We were to take turns covering County's Emergency Room (ER). He said, "Okay. All of you have to take a month covering County ER." One guy in the group said no. He was nervous and thought he'd be no good at it, and he just wasn't going to do it.

We understood, sort of. County *was* kind of scary. All the trauma went there: car accidents, assaults...sometimes patients would stop at the ER on their way to jail with arresting officers in tow. Sometimes that patient would take a swing at you. You'd hit the floor, look up, and there the patient would be with two cops on top of him. It was surreal sometimes. Once in a while a well-dressed businessman would come in and ask for a shot of penicillin. "Well, I don't *know* that I have anything wrong, but I had a kind of wild night last night... and well, you know." We'd give him the shot. Medicine is a service industry, after all.

After the anxious intern's refusal in Sully's living room, the good doctor got everyone another beer and we discussed it some more. Then he disappeared into his basement. When he came back up, his pant legs were rolled up to the knees. His basement had flooded, but he was interested in keeping the discussion going at the same time. This is just kind of how he lived his life. After a while, the rest of the group decided we would all take a few extra days of the County coverage. The other guy did some special project to make up for it. And Sully got on with pumping out his basement.

My shift covering County coincided with the July 1966 race riots. In those days, north Omaha was almost exclusively black and poor. There were federal housing projects, surrounded by substandard schools, no after-school programs, many churches, but little else. Opportunity to get out of the cycle of poverty existed, but it was very difficult. Many residents felt angry and stuck. Things like the Civil Rights Act of 1964 and the Voting Rights Act of 1965 seemed to be having no impact in their lives. And then a heat wave settled over the city. On July 4, a large group of young people hanging out on the corner of 24th and Lake Street was confronted by police, who were trying to disperse them. That seemed to be one insult too many. The anger and frustration just sort of blew up. They destroyed those two police cars, hurled Molotov cocktails through windows, demolished storefronts up and down Lake Street.

I was about two miles away at the County ER, scared to death. I knew there were enormous fires. I imagined I would be treating major burns, deep lacerations, battlefield-type injuries... But no one came. The emergency room sat empty all night except for two motorcycle cops that had gotten scraped up in an accident. One of the biggest nights of rioting in Nebraska history, and I treated no one. It was disturbing. The National Guard had been called in, and they set up a perimeter. Fire engines and ambulances had tried to get into the fray, but retreated after being shot at. They refused to re-enter the area.

I do not have a solution for the social and racial problems of our country. In many ways, it seems that today we are reliving the conflicts of the 1960s or the 1920s.

People seem to want to blame others: the authorities, the wealthy, the immigrants, and especially the angry poor. As I have said before, I do believe that everyone really wants to make something special of his or her life and, given an opportunity and a vision, will work hard to make it happen. However, I also believe that people can be defeated, especially from lack of opportunity, and lose energy.

In my later years as a Creighton faculty member, I had a resident who said she did not like the patients at the Veteran's Administration because so many just want to get handouts. I was not pleased with her remark and attitude for many reasons. One reason was that our veterans have served their country and have a right to the healthcare and other benefits that they have been promised. However, my dissatisfaction ran deeper. She seemed to have no insight that many of the patients in the veterans healthcare system are poor, have been defeated in many ways by life, and are just trying to get by any way they can. My student was an immigrant, intelligent, very hard working, and determined to be successful, but I think she was overlooking her privilege. Those who are born with opportunity should recognize and appreciate it. And they should know that not everyone has opportunity. She was a physician. I expected more from her.

I did discuss my opinions with her. When I said, "I believe that everyone wants to make something of their life," she said, "That's a nice way to look at the world." I am not sure I changed her opinion about the patients at the VA. But whether they want to rise up or not isn't the point. Everyone *deserves* an opportunity to make something of his life.

Martzie and I were married in September 1966 in Sioux City, Iowa. The reception was at her home with lots of family. My mother was very happy, especially after Monsignor Flanagan got her alone and told her that the Braungers were a wonderful family. I thought it was very thoughtful of the old Irish priest to reassure my mother about those Germans. It was a happy day.

VIII – Full Circle

Most of my internship year was served at St. Joseph's hospital. I was on call one night that winter when I got a call. The nurse on the phone said, "We've got a guy who's all agitated down here. Give me something to sedate him so he will calm down, because he's just raising hell. We are going to move him to the psych ward."

I figured I'd better do an examination if I was going to be prescribing sedatives, so I went down there to look at him. I glanced at his chart and stopped in my tracks. Just down the hallway, making a terrible ruckus, sat L.J. DeBacker, the same doctor who had delivered me. This was my sister Pat's father-in-law, the man who treated not only me as a child, but also my dad. Dr. DeBacker prescribed all those medications for my dad and kept him alive in his last years. This was the same man who wrote my recommendation to medical school—possibly he was the reason I was even standing there that day. I couldn't have been more shocked.

The nurse shared what she knew about this new patient. "He's a doc somewhere outstate—Hastings, I think. He was in the hospital out there because he's in kidney failure, and they can't control him. He gets up and goes home any time he wants 'cause he's practiced in that hospital all his life. If he wants to go for lunch, he goes home for lunch. They shipped him here so we can treat him and maybe keep better control of him."

I wandered down the hall and I could hear him hollering the whole way. I walked into the room, and I looked at him.

"Dr. DeBacker," I said.

"Yeah?"

"Do you know who I am?"

He looked at me and blinked for a minute. Then he said, "You're Joe."

"That's right. What's going on? They tell me you're raising hell and they want me to give you something to put you to sleep. What's the matter?"

"I don't want to die in a psych ward."

The stillness in the room was palpable. Of course this distinguished man didn't want to die with the indignity of being labeled a psychiatric patient. Dr. DeBacker already seemed calmer. He finally had someone listening, someone who understood him and respected him.

"If I cancel the order to transfer you to the psych ward, will you behave?"

"Absolutely. You won't hear another thing from me."

So, I consulted with his urologist and together we agreed to give him another chance and see how he did.

About 1:00 that morning the phone rang and woke me up. "We got a guy over here to pronounce. You're the intern on call." That meant I needed to go verify death and pronounce someone dead. That's true of anyone who dies in a hospital. It's just part of the job.

I got up, wandered down there and it was Dr. DeBacker who had died. *Wow. Circle of life*, I thought. *This man delivered me, and now I am pronouncing him dead*. It was bittersweet, but I felt glad that I had cancelled his transfer and let him die in peace. Neither of us knew just hours before how close to death he was, but his final wish had been granted...by me. I felt like I had done something good and allowed him some dignity.

As an intern, I shuffled bodily fluids all day. So when I walked a urine sample into the lab one day and asked for it to be tested for pregnancy, no one batted an eye. When the tech said, "It's positive," my response was, "All right!"

"First kid, huh?"

Yes. Yes, indeed, I thought to myself. *I am going to be a father.* It was an ah-ha moment in my life. I was happy there would be a child soon. It felt like an opportunity to carry on the family's legacy. No longer a child, I would now be a parent. It was a little scary, but exciting.

Chapter 6

Mayo Clinic, 1967-1970

I – Residency

The next step on my road to being a full-fledged physician was to serve a residency in internal medicine. While interning at Creighton, an attending physician suggested I follow his path and apply to the Mayo Clinic in Rochester, Minnesota for those three years. So I did. I was tickled when they accepted me, though I didn't quite realize that by accepting the position, I would be taking a pay cut for the privilege. I had been making $4,800 per year in Omaha; my work in Rochester netted $4,000. The reason was supply and demand, I was told. The more desirable and competitive a residency is, the less they pay the residents. During my first year at Mayo, a list was published in *Postgraduate Medicine* ranking the country's residencies by student preference. Mayo Clinic was number one on the desirability list. Lucky me.

The Mayo Clinic was founded by Drs. Will and Charlie Mayo shortly before the turn of the twentieth century. They put patient care first, second, and third, followed by education and research. I loved that approach. Caring for people on a connected, human level seems obvious to me. We are here to serve others. It's the only way to practice medicine, in my opinion. That's not how everyone does it, though, so I was grateful to be working in an environment that resonated with my values.

Mayo's quirks extended beyond patient care. They did many things differently, including calling their resident physicians "fellows." Technically speaking, I was never a resident physician, but I was a fellow twice. And, I discovered, I would not be wearing a white doctor's coat. The doctors, Charlie and Will, felt it created an artificial barrier between doctors and patients. They wore suit coats, and so, 75 years later, I would also be wearing a suit coat.

I hadn't gotten that memo. I had just moved my pregnant wife and all our worldly belongings four hundred miles to our new home. And now I needed a suit, pronto. I ran downtown to the men's clothing store, walked in the front door, and before I said a word, the guy behind the counter said, "You one of those new fellows?"

"Yeah."

"And...let me guess. You want a suit. One suit that looks good, that you can wear every day for three years and nobody notices that it's the same suit."

I laughed and said, "You got it."

I was told my new suit was brown. (I wouldn't know brown from green.) But I remember it was a nice suit—nice but not too nice, you know? Respectable, but not putting on airs...and I wouldn't cry if someone bled on it. It didn't take long to adjust to this new way of presenting myself. Everyone else was wearing the same thing too.

Quirks aside, I admired the Mayo Clinic's way of doing things. They're the most organized place you've ever been. There is a system for everything. Because of that organization, they manage to provide care to many thousands of people each year. One reason they can do so is most of their patients are outpatients. Other hospitals have to admit those people, but Mayo does not because their system is so good. I learned a lot from my time there.

II – Mari

On November 24, 1967, Martzie and I rushed off to St. Mary's Hospital in Rochester. Our first child was about to be born. In those days, fathers were not included in the birth process, not even fathers who were doctors. So, I sat in the waiting room with the other men. Though this was many years before ultrasound would be used to determine gender, I had a feeling this baby was a girl. And then, the delivering physician brought out my baby girl! "She has red hair," he said.

I remember holding this new person and wondering where in the world she had come from. Just days before, there had only been two members in our household. And now we were three. But it also felt right. I had always assumed I would be a father, and now I was. We named her Maureen Cecilia Lynch, Mari for short. That nickname stuck so well, I doubt if many of Mari's friends over the years knew that she had a different name. It was just right for my girl.

When Martzie and I brought Mari home, it seemed like there was more work than two people could reasonably accomplish. For me, there were hours at the hospital, hours in the classroom, spending time with my wife and daughter, and I had to study somewhere in there too. It seemed in those days like I was always working, studying, or feeling guilty that I wasn't studying. The housing complex we lived in helped some. We fellows were all in the same boat. The little houses were built in a round oval, front doors all facing a grassy courtyard. So we could hang out in the front yard, leave the door open, and still hear a baby waking from a nap. In fact you could hear other people's babies waking too. So, it was possible to make a run to the store during naptime and ask a neighbor to keep an ear open for you. That little community of people made the workload a bit easier for us.

Sometimes we would get a sitter and head out to watch a play. Rochester had a wonderful playhouse; all the fellows and spouses enjoyed going there for a night out. I admired it so much that I was shocked when the director quit and moved to Omaha, home of the country's largest community theater center. I had no idea that resource was in my old backyard.

All the neighbors enjoyed camaraderie. When the landlord raised the rent every year, we would band together and march down to argue with him. We never won. He knew we wouldn't be there long, and he wasn't reliant on our repeat business. There would be a new crop of fellows the next year.

Martzie got a job as a Medical Technologist at Olmstead Community Hospital. I remember she was very proud to be invited to work in the nation's best medical community. I was happy for her. It meant she would be utilizing her Creighton degree, which made her happy. But it also meant that we had to juggle childcare. My schedule was nuts, and I was often on call. That was hard, and it caused some conflict between us. It seemed like we just couldn't get in sync about how to split our duties up.

The push-pull, never-enough-time feeling of a family's early years is hard. It's a time in life when everything seems to be happening at once, and you never feel like you're covering all the bases. But I remember beautiful moments as well. Because of my night-owl study habits, I was often the one who comforted Mari when she cried in the night. Holding her, feeding her, gazing at her bright little eyes in the darkened house, I fell in love with that girl.

III – Vietnam

Around the time that I came to Rochester, the country was trying to build up enough manpower to fight in Vietnam, and they were really short on doctors. Thus, the military was especially interested in medical school graduates like me and my fellow interns. The class of 1966 medical school graduates were drafted into the Army unless they had obtained a deferment. I applied for a Berry Plan deferment in the Navy, and was fortunate enough to receive a three-year deferment to finish my residency training before going on active duty. The whole time I was working away at the Mayo Clinic, the specter of Vietnam lurked on my horizon. I wasn't able to make future plans or apply for any subspecialty training slots because I knew my time was already spoken for. The Marines didn't have a medical corps, so the Navy supported their medical needs. I was sworn in by the Navy, and started making plans to move Martzie and Mari somewhere so I could attend basic training and then ship out.

Then one morning, I opened the newspaper to a headline that read, *Nixon Orders Troop Withdrawal.* Sixty thousand Marines were being pulled out of Vietnam. The conflict was winding down, and I hadn't set foot on foreign soil. A week later, I got a letter from the Navy stating that the Marines had been pulled out of Vietnam, they were much overstaffed with physicians, and I had two options. I could transfer to the Army or Air Force and go on active duty, or I could stay in the Navy Reserve for six years. I said, "I love the Navy!"

I remember feeling very relieved. And also guilty. It seemed like every guy my age, everyone I grew up with and went to med school with, had gone to serve his country. Being a Midwesterner, service to God and country are as deeply embedded in my character as church on Sunday followed by pot roast. It's who I was raised to be. To have stayed home in relative safety while my fellow interns and high school friends were getting shot at was a little upsetting. As I recall, I was the only intern at Creighton who didn't go into the military. I stayed home. All of them came back alive, thank goodness, though a high school friend was killed while piloting a plane. He was shot down.

Add to that, the climate in the country was turbulent. People's patience with the conflict was running out as it dragged on and on. At the beginning of the war, I supported the effort. I equated patriotism with support of the military because that's what good citizens thought. But I was wrong.

Sometime during those years, I went to San Francisco. I stood there on Market Street and watched the anti-war protests. Everybody was chanting, "LBJ, LBJ! How many babies did you kill today?" I remember standing there next to a soldier in uniform, looking at him and wondering what that must feel like, to have your welcome home marred by a backdrop of protesters. What was it like to have kids you once considered friends shouting such angry words about your service?

And then I flew back to Omaha. Next to the airport was a billboard, "Support Your Fighting Men." The discord was uncomfortable. *This is gonna make me schizophrenic,* I thought. It took me years, but I eventually decided I could do both things. I could support the troops who fought for our country, but vehemently disagree with the men who sent them away.

I was in the Navy Reserve for six years. I never once went to a meeting. Never attended a training camp. Never owned a uniform. And yet, I got promoted every two years. On paper I was a Lieutenant Commander in the Navy Reserve, but I knew absolutely nothing about military service. I thought it was a little scary. *How many people in the Reserves know nothing, like me?* I wondered.

Every so often, the Navy Reserve Medical Corps would write me a letter and ask if I would start a unit up in Omaha. They didn't have one there. I would always write back explaining that I was woefully under-qualified for such a duty. "I do not think I am the appropriate person to begin a unit." Their response was always something like, "Well, thanks anyway. We appreciate your input."

Many years later, during the medical school class of 1966's 50th year reunion, I stood up and said I wanted to thank my classmates for their service in Vietnam because I knew no one thanked them then. Afterwards, a couple of them came up to me and told me that I was right, no one had ever thanked them until that day when I did.

IV – Coming Home

When the Navy said I was assigned to the Reserves, rather than active duty, I was happy. I was also out of a job. I hadn't made any plans post-residency. As an official internist, I considered maybe returning to the Pacific Northwest. I had enjoyed living there, but there was a recession crushing the economy. It seemed like a bad time to be going into practice there.

So I called up Creighton and asked if there was any room in their cardiology fellowship. I had been thinking about specializing in cardiology during my internal medicine rotation. Maybe it was because my father died from heart disease, but mostly I think it was because cardiology always seemed to me to be the most fascinating and fun area of medicine.

In May 1970, I sent my records, an application for the Cardiovascular Diseases Fellowship, and a letter of recommendation to Dr. Richard Booth, Chief of Cardiology at Creighton University School of Medicine. He called me and invited me to come to Omaha to look things over. During my June visit, I found Dr. Booth making rounds at the hospital and stopped him in the hall. It was a three-second conversation during which he said, "Love to have you. Your records are fine."

I was so relieved. It was extremely late in the year to be finding a position. Usually, these arrangements were made at least six to twelve months ahead of time. Again, luck was in my favor. There were some administrative problems at Creighton that meant they hadn't yet filled the fellowship, and it was mine if I wanted it. I started in three weeks.

So, I headed back to Rochester to help Martzie pack up. She was pregnant with our second child, and we were both happy to be returning to familiar ground to establish our family. Back to Omaha we went!

Chapter 7

A Growing Family

I – Omaha & a Son

Mari was almost three when we moved back to Omaha in July 1970. It took a few months to get settled into my new/old role as a Fellow studying cardiovascular diseases. It was good to be back at Creighton University School of Medicine and great to be working with many of my old friends again. I remember feeling a little overwhelmed as I walked the familiar streets of Omaha. The last time I had lived there, my time was largely devoted to work. Now that I had a wife and a little girl at home, I felt a little divided between wanting to be with them and knowing I had to put in the hours at work too. I loved both things and there never seemed to be enough time.

When I was at home, I loved watching Mari tumble around the house. With her curly red hair and her fearless nature, she ran full speed everywhere like a grinning fire bolt. Suddenly, there was a whole new energy in our home. I liked it, but it was also sobering. Having children makes you suddenly aware of your own mortality. When Mari was first born, I remember fearing what could happen to us. What if she were hurt? What if I was hurt and left her alone? What if her mother were hurt? What would I do if this little girl were left solely in my care? I knew nothing about little girls. I didn't know how to fix hair, especially not curly hair. I didn't know how to play dolls, or how to make sense of all the layers of girl clothing. I knew about throwing a ball around, but what would I do with a little girl?

I learned as Mari grew that parenting doesn't really require prerequisite skills. Children teach you what they need from you. If you don't know how to do an important task, you learn. I figured out how to change diapers. I learned that I loved bottle-feeding babies. And I knew I wanted my kids to be readers, so I read with all the children as they grew.

Mari was a climber. Sometimes my father's heart leapt as she scaled up greater and greater heights. One time when she was older, maybe five, I looked up and saw her teetering much higher than she should have been. Mari was attempting to balance on top of the A-frame swing set in our neighbor's yard. Fearful, I stood up and started running toward her. "Don't move!" As I raced, Mari wobbled, and then slipped off that set. It seemed to be happening in slow motion. Then, just before I could catch her, Mari hit the ground and cut her forehead. She was crying, I felt like crying, and she was bleeding all over the place. After the stitches, I remember replaying that moment over and over in my head. It was troubling and a little shocking to me that I hadn't been able to protect Mari—and I had been right there. Protecting is what dads are supposed to do, after all. But I couldn't shield her from that pain. It was a lesson I would learn over and over again.

Another time, perhaps a year or so later, Mari fell from another epic climb, catching her weight with a palm to the ground. It looked like a hard fall, but there didn't seem to be any swelling. My thoughts turned to all those hours I had worked in hospital emergency rooms. Worried parents often brought their kids in for x-rays. Most of the time, they were normal. So I figured the odds were good that Mari's wrist would be fine. To distract her from this sad episode, I suggested her favorite diversion: putt-putt golf! She put on a brave face and tried to believe me, that the pain in her wrist was no big deal.

But when we began playing, Mari started crying when she tried to putt. That's when I knew we should be in an emergency room, not out golfing. I felt like a dolt. It can be so hard to tell the difference between tears of pain and tears of protest, but these tears were clear. We went and got that x-ray. And then a cast.

Before all that climbing, Mari was a happy toddler. Because she was so young when we were preparing to bring her brother into the world, I'm not sure she fully understood or was even aware why her mother's lap kept shrinking. The abstraction, "You're going to be a big sister," probably didn't mean much to her at age three.

Michael Francis Lynch was born at St. Joseph's Hospital on November 23 in 1970. His middle name, Francis, was after Martzie's father. I remember Mike being a calm baby. It was around his infancy that I took up the family role of rocker-in-chief. I was often up at night with calls anyway, so it was easy for me to take a few extra minutes and rock a fussy baby back to sleep. Our home had a wooden rocking chair in the living room. If I was home for evening bedtime, I would gather up whoever needed to be put to sleep and start rocking slowly. I enjoyed holding Mike while he dozed, eyelids fluttering, his milky breath getting slower and slower. Mike was warm in the chill of the November night. It was like holding a peaceful little furnace.

With two children, the house seemed more than twice as loud. It's funny how that works. As Mike and Mari grew, they palled around together. Sometimes, the kids went to the babysitter during the day. Then at night we would all return home to the rental where we lived, and the house would be filled again with dinner sounds, gentle bickering from tired children, bath time, then stories. I remember when

Mike was preschool age, some evenings his peacefulness would run out and insecurity would take over. He was a gentle person—still is—and the world seemed too overwhelming for his three-year-old self to bear any longer. He would cry with a bone-tired weariness not usually seen in someone so young. It broke my heart. Dark closets, mean kids, scratchy pajamas, the peas at dinner all worked against him as he tried to relax and go to sleep. So I would gently rub his back, and try to comfort him. "It will be okay. You will wake up in the morning and you will feel better. You'll see." The next morning, Mike's smile would rise with the sun and he would bound out of bed looking forward to his day, no matter how early it started. His laugh was something I came to count on as he grew and developed a great sense of humor.

II – Mom

Not long after Mike was born, my mom had a stroke. She was admitted to St. Joseph's Hospital in Omaha. I was glad to be back in town where I could see her every day and keep track of her progress. I certainly saw her as my mother, not as my patient. Fortunately, she was primarily taken care of by one of my neurology friends. Mom did have some residual weakness in her left arm and hand, and for months she constantly squeezed a small rubber ball to gain strength and dexterity. She didn't suffer too much damage from the stroke, but was frail enough that I didn't want her going back home to live alone until she regained some muscle strength and balance. She had been living in a small house she bought in Grand Island, not far from Pat.

After she was dismissed from the hospital she stayed with us for a while. She enjoyed reading to Mari. I considered keeping her in our home, but it wasn't an ideal solution. There were stairs, which were difficult for her, and Martzie had all she could handle with her work and the kids. I knew there was going to have to be a nursing home, and I knew Mom wasn't going to like it. Who would? So I attempted a pep talk.

"What you have to do, Mom, is decide whether you believe me. If you believe me, you have the power to make this a short stay. You'll go in that nursing home for the winter and get stronger, and then I'll take you back home. Or, if you think this is just a setup to stick you in the nursing home forever, you won't get better."

She said, "I'm going to the nursing home, and I'm going home in the spring." And she did, and we did. A winter's worth of physical therapy was enough to help my 74-year-old mother regain stability and independence. She went home to Grand Island where Pat and her 11 children could visit her regularly. Mom loved being near them. I think the thought of going home to them and to her house helped her power through all the hard work.

She loved that little house on John Street. A few years earlier when she decided to move back to Grand Island from Toppenish, Pat and I tried to find her a place to live. We showed her an apartment next to St. Mary's church. She walked in, turned around and walked out. Pat and I followed her quietly as she walked out the door and down the street. We got in the car and she said firmly, "I am not going to be one of the old women by the church." And that was that. She eventually bought the house on John Street.

Through that winter, I got a chance to visit my mom regularly. It had been a while since we had talked so much and I was grateful for the opportunity to see her, though it could be awkward sometimes. We didn't always have much to talk about, so we talked about the old days when I was young. She would bring up stories or people, and I couldn't remember them. She would mention one name after another, and I couldn't recall them. It was odd, since she was 74 and I was 28. If anyone should have been having problems with focus, it was her. But Mom was generous about my memory lapses. She said, "You have the most wonderful convenient memory of anybody I know, Joe. I would give anything to have a memory like yours. You remember only the good things."

I suppose she was right. There's a lot about my life that has been lost to time. Some of that's to be expected. I'm not sure where other memories disappear to. I do try to dwell on the things I am grateful for, not the parts of my life I dislike. I believe that ruminating on fears and anger makes those things worse. So, I try to hold onto the special, warm memories and let the rest go.

Mom lived contentedly in her Grand Island home for four more years before passing away in 1974. She was happy to be surrounded by her grandchildren and children in her last years. Though I miss her still, her influence in my life lives on in the way I parent and grandparent, in the way I view the world, in the way I try to be of service. If I could sum her life philosophy up in one idea, I would say, "Be nice." Regardless of people's background or circumstances, Mom taught me to be kind.

III – The End of School

All along in my medical training, I had been traveling an intuitive path, unsure where I would end up, but feeling my way toward what seemed to be the best match for my interests and skills. Internal medicine residents have the opportunity to do subspecialty training in fields like gastroenterology, respiratory diseases, etc. For me, the heart was and is fascinating. It's so intricate and yet so powerful. It affects the entire body, and its function and actions totally make sense to me. Cardiology is a very large and exciting field that is always changing and advancing rapidly.

I loved doing my fellowship training at Creighton. In that teaching setting, I was able to not only care for patients; I got to work with other doctors in training. I loved being a part of a team of professionals putting their heads together to find the best possible outcome for each patient. It's fast-paced work. In some ways it's a young man's game because St. Joseph's, Douglas County and the VA were hospitals that saw many poor patients and very sick patients. From the physician perspective, it can be kind of exciting if you're up for it. Every day there is a new emergency, a new technique to study, an innovation happening around every corner. At age 30, it was exactly where I wanted to be.

In 1972, I was pleased when the Creighton School of Medicine offered me a permanent position as a cardiologist. I said yes with no hesitation. I would now be able to continue in that team environment, responsible for patients at the clinic and the hospital, as well as teaching younger doctors-in-training. In some ways, I didn't really leave school until I retired at age 74. I have loved being a part of Creighton.

IV -- Early years at Creighton Cardiology

I spent my entire professional career with Creighton Cardiology. Mostly, I saw patients, made rounds at the hospital and taught medical students, residents, and fellows. However, when I began in the Division of Cardiology, I was assigned an additional duty, to direct our phone line electrocardiogram (EKG) interpretation system.

In the 1960s the Chief of Cardiology, Dr. Richard Booth, along with John Glaser and others, had begun a program of reading EKGs for rural hospitals. I believe they were the first cardiology group to read EKGs, 24 hours a day, 7 days a week, transmitted via phone lines. At its peak, there were well over 100 hospitals and clinics involved over a nine-state area. With the expansion of cardiology groups and the advent of computerized EKGs, the need for phone-line EKG interpretation has decreased.

John Glaser was also an airplane pilot and we would travel throughout the area for a number of weeks each year, visiting the various hospital administrators, physicians, and medical personnel. Usually we enjoyed it, but it could get tiresome. Once, John tried to go through an innocent-looking cloud in South Dakota and we were suddenly engulfed in a loud, frightening hailstorm. Another time, we were almost hit by a crop duster that apparently didn't see us and suddenly cut in front of us while we were landing in Grafton, North Dakota. I never got used to landing on a grass strip in Rolla, North Dakota near the Canadian border. Sometimes, we had trusting souls we worked with that would just leave a car at the airport, and tell us where the key was so we could drive ourselves to the hospital.

Some places were very special, such as the small hospitals in Oakes and Hankinson, North Dakota, where the sisters of St. Francis were always very welcoming.

In the 1970s our cardiology group began outreach clinics, regularly visiting to see patients, who were referred by local physicians. John and I did a regular overnight trip, initially driving three and one-half hours to Burwell, Nebraska for a clinic, and then going on to another clinic that evening, sixty miles farther in Bassett, Nebraska. Sometimes we stayed overnight at the Bassett Lodge, but usually we drove twenty miles farther west for another clinic in Atkinson the next morning.

On the way, we would stop to eat at a bar/restaurant near Newport, Nebraska. By the time we arrived the kitchen was usually closed but they would open it for us. John and I would order the same thing to make the cook's job a little easier, hamburger steak with Heinz 57 steak sauce and tater tots. I would have one beer, but John never touched alcohol. For a number of years we would get gas on a side street in Newport where a single gas pump stood in front of a home. We would fill up with gas and then leave the appropriate amount of money in a box inside the screened-in porch. We would usually leave a little extra.

If we had time, we would slip over to Long Pine, Nebraska, a few miles west of Bassett, which was a small community in a steep valley. It had a stream with houses beside it. We might visit Tom Gallagher, a bachelor who had a place next to the stream for his nieces and nephews to visit. He had an organ in his living room that he sometimes played for us.

In the 1970s, my associate, Dr. Syed Mohiuddin, and I began going to an outreach clinic at Myrtue Memorial Hospital in Harlan, Iowa. A few years later we also began a cardiology clinic at Cass County Hospital in Atlantic, Iowa. We continued to go to Harlan and Atlantic for over 30 years.

These travels gave me a special opportunity to appreciate the beauty and uniqueness of the countryside, communities and especially the people of the rural Midwest. In 2015 John and I made a trip together for a few days, "for old times' sake," to a number of these communities and enjoyed visiting and reminiscing with old friends.

Looking back, I think I had the best job in the world. I was able to practice medicine, hang around a university with all its energy and dynamism, and still make a good living. I was always allowed and encouraged to pursue anything I wanted to do, whether it was spending more time teaching medical students or spending much of the summer in the Dominican Republic as a part of the Creighton University Institute for Latin American Concern (ILAC) healthcare program. Sometimes, a pay adjustment might have been necessary for that time away, but that was fine with me. I was always treated fairly.

Throughout my life, I felt I was surrounded by the best and brightest, from grade school friends to teachers, colleagues, and patients. For the most part, during our time together, they just carried me along with them.

V – Now We Are Five

On September 5, 1975 we had a red-haired baby boy, our third child, also born at St. Joseph's Hospital. Martzie and I had been using traditional and family names up until then, but we had taken a liking to a new boy's name that we thought was pretty original, Ryan. It wasn't until later that we realized we were on the front end of a trend of Ryans that would last over a decade. We thought we were being original, but apparently, so did thousands of other couples. His middle name was Patrick after my father.

When he was still small, I kept up my rocking chair duties with Ryan. By then, Mike and Mari were old enough to catch on to my magical trick. I nearly always got my lap-sitting companion to sleep. "Daaad..." they teased, "you don't do anything. You just keep rocking no matter what, until he gives up. You're really just boring him to sleep." Some call it boring; I call it genius.

Ryan Patrick Lynch is special in many ways. His energy is boundless; he is always looking for opportunities. As a kid, I remember him selling lemonade or making declarations about what he was going to do. Goal-driven, we could call him. Ryan also loved nature. He used to stare out our kitchen window at the beautiful backyard that Martzie encouraged along. "Aren't those flowers beautiful?" he would say. He was the only kid I ever knew who thought to marvel at landscaping. It struck me because I'm not sure until then that I had even noticed the blooms.

He had a special knack for finding lost things. Anytime I misplaced my wallet, my car keys, a book, anything, I would ask him to find it for me. As I recall, he always found the missing object. I considered this amazing. Since I constantly lost things, Ryan's special ability was very helpful to me.

Ryan enjoyed acting but peaked out rather early with the lead role of Ichabod Crane in the fifth-grade production of *The Legend of Sleepy Hollow*. He worked hard most of the time during summers in college, at Walgreens, Shopko, and the zoo. He also had an internship at the *Omaha World Herald*. I thought the most interesting of those was his job at the zoo as a tram tour guide, announcing all the fascinating details of the animals and exhibits as the tram snaked through the zoo. I thought he was very good and knowledgeable. He took pride in the details. During high school he did spend a few weeks living on a farm in Galway with a host family and traveling around Ireland. The Irish said he fit in perfectly with his red hair, Irish features and heritage, and with the name Ryan Patrick Lynch.

To my great sadness, I wasn't there as much for Ryan's teen years, but we spent as many weekends and days together as possible. Fortunately, Ryan was a really good teenager and didn't really require my night owl duties. Though I was living separately, I still found ways to see him often. For instance, I picked Ryan up early the mornings when he had 7:00 a.m. band practice. My routine was to drive through McDonald's for a cinnamon roll and orange juice that he could eat in the car between his house and Creighton Prep. It was our special time. Ryan played a great French horn in concert band at Creighton Prep High School. I remember attending one concert when he surprised me by stepping up to the podium and delivering a very polished speech. I thought he was already pretty well grown up.

Just like my bookish mother, I wanted my own children to love to read. As they grew, I tried to read to them or have them read to me as much as I could. I felt the best time was at bedtime because it was uninterrupted quiet. Plus, they were eager to go on as long as possible so they wouldn't have to turn off the light and go to sleep. Sometimes I would say it was time to go to bed earlier than necessary so we had extra time. Clearly, I looked forward to it.

They liked it too. My plan was to get them to love listening, then pointing at pictures, and gradually get better at reading. As they got a little older, I would choose books for them to read independently. I did not feel that the literary merit of the books was important at all at the beginning. The most important thing initially was to get them hooked. Once I felt they were pretty well hooked on books, I would encourage them to read better books, to move up in challenge and length.

When Mike was younger, he and I spent quite a bit of time together in the evenings. We worked on homework and then we would take turns reading at bedtime. I came across the Narnia books by C.S. Lewis and we went through most of the series. I found that I was as interested in the stories as he was. I am so proud of the work Mike put into his academics. I know it wasn't always fun, but he never complained and his work really paid off. He's one of the hardest workers I know and his career successes are proof of his talent.

Not too long ago Mari shared with me how my literacy plan worked for her. When she was about a junior in high school she signed up for an elective English class, which was just reading and discussing assigned books for a semester. According to her memory, on the first day of the class when she was given the reading list for the semester, she discovered that she had already read every single book on the list. "I didn't even know you were giving me the classics to read," she said proudly.

None of the kids were any trouble during their teenage years. Mari worked at Younkers Department Store. She did like to stay out late. When I told her, "Nothing good happens after 1:00 a.m.," she said, "I don't even get off work from Younkers until nearly 11:00 p.m. Things are just getting started then." She did seem to always make it home nearly on time. I never could go to sleep until the kids got home. When I was living at home, I would wait until after they quietly went up the stairs and went to bed. Then, I would go into their room and give them a kiss on their forehead to let them know I knew they were home.

Probably due to her late nights, Mari could always sleep in. (She still does that.) She did it so much the family started calling her Garfield. One school morning, I decided that I wasn't going to wake her up multiple times, like I had been doing every morning. I tried once or twice and then gave up. At 1:00 p.m., Mari finally awoke on her own and was shocked, then mad. She had missed a test at school. From then on, she did better in the mornings.

Mari also enjoyed traveling and spent a month living with a host family in Bilbao, in the Basque country of northern Spain, studying Spanish and learning the culture. Later, one of the girls from this host family visited us in Omaha. The Spanish came in handy when she volunteered one summer as a Creighton student in the Dominican Republic, as an *ayudante* or helper, with the ILAC health care summer team.

Every summer, our family would try to take a vacation somewhere. It didn't have to be fancy, but I thought it was important for the family to have time together, just us. As a boy, I enjoyed the camping trips to the Snowy Range in Wyoming with my sister and the rest of the DeBackers, and I wanted my own children to see more of the country. We thought about camping, but I agreed with Martzie that it's not much of a break for the family cook, who has to work even harder outside of a kitchen. So, we found other outdoorsy locales with amenities like Yellowstone National Park; Door County, Wisconsin; Fort Robinson State Park in Nebraska and the Black Hills of South Dakota.

One special spot was Eaton's Ranch, Wyoming. It was a dude ranch with cabins and activities every day. Each guest was assigned a horse for the week. When the wranglers asked me if we had any experience with horses, I said none at all. We really didn't, and I wanted to be safe. The horses they gave us were so gentle and slow, you might even call them lazy. They kind of plodded along. Ryan, who had long ago graduated from the rocking chair, fell asleep as his horse slowly loped along the trail one evening. He was sitting there one minute, and then kind of humped forward, and he sort of just slid off the saddle and onto the ground, where he promptly woke up wondering what in the heck happened! If I could go back and have that conversation with the wrangler again, I would say we had *a little* experience with horses so we might get some with more spunk.

Some of the most important and meaningful activities for our family were things we happened upon by chance. Soapbox derby was that way for us. If you've never seen it, soapbox derby is car racing for kids. In the very beginning of the sport (1930s or so) the cars were literally made from wooden soap crates and baby buggy wheels. Modern derby cars are made from kits, but are still powered by gravity. The kids can get going pretty fast, sometimes up to 35 miles an hour as they race downhill.

Since it had been well established by then that I was not a handy sort of fellow, I was more than grateful to Martzie's brother-in-law,

Roger VanWaart, and his brother Jerry, when they offered to help our three kids build their derby car kits. From assembling the shell to packing the wheel bearings, Roger and Jerry have always been there to ensure it was done correctly.

Mari only got to race one year, and sadly, we weren't as practiced at car building then. On race day, the car malfunctioned and she was eliminated. By the next year she was too old to participate. Mike and Ryan both had very successful soapbox derby careers. Both of them won state championships, facilitating the purchase of a GMC van to transport their cars.

We called that painted van The Rolling Total. We used it on road trips for years, transporting derby cars and kids to their races around the region. Usually, these trips included cousins and hotels with pools with lots of splashing at night when the racing was done. I have many wonderful memories of unwinding at the end of a long day with Roger. He and I would enjoy a beer while the kids laughed and played with their cousins in the pool.

Mike and Ryan both made it to soapbox derby nationals in Akron, Ohio. Ryan earned his way to Akron twice, in junior division in 1986 and in senior division in 1987. In the national races in Akron, they race three cars at a time, so it is a real accomplishment to win races against the other area champions as both Mike and Ryan did. Mike even placed fourth in the All American nationals in Akron in 1982. There was a great picture of him in the *World Herald* newspaper that showed him in his seat with only the helmet peeking above the car.

Standing on the sidelines cheering for my kids or grandkids is one of my favorite things to do. That's why it tickles me to see the family tradition carrying on to my grandchildren's generation, with Roger and Jerry's continuing help and support. The family time spent on tournament days is invaluable. And it's an honor and a joy to have been a part of its beginnings.

Mari, Mike and Ryan all played soccer, and I enjoyed watching them run up and down the field. I was lucky enough to have the flexibility at work that I could usually work my schedule around the kids' activities and could make it to most of their programs and games.

Sometimes, Mike played goalie. One game against a strong St. Robert's team ended tied 0 to 0; he was fierce in the goal. Mike was proud he had held them scoreless. At the end of the shutout, he blocked a shot and then slammed the ball down into the turf. It bounced back up, far into the air, tracing an arc across the blue sky.

One other soccer memory has stuck with me for many years. When Mike was 7, he had the kindest coach. The man was a South African with the loveliest Queen's English accent. The ball rolled up to Mike and he stutter-stepped a bit, trying to position himself to kick with his dominant right foot.

Coach said, "Mike, you should kick the ball with your left foot."

Mike replied, "Oh, I'm not so good at that."

"Ah, but you must try," the coach answered. That short sentence turned on a light bulb in my head. *Yes!* I thought. Just like biochemistry, some things in life are harder than others, but you must try anyway. I have repeated that phrase over and over—both to my kids and to myself—when circumstances have been hard.

My impression is that, over the years, the kids and I have gotten along very well and enjoyed each other, even though we all know I am grouchy sometimes. I know I still enjoy and respect them today. They continue to like to tease me. They laughingly give me real and fake hugs, with comments like "I love you, man," knowing I am awkward with that.

They still make fun of how I taught them to drive. First, driving around in a large parking lot like at Burke High School, then on streets, then bigger streets, and finally learning to merge and drive on highways and interstates. They laugh as they recall how nervous I was. Mari enjoys recalling how I unconsciously ate a number of the large chocolate bars schools used to sell for fundraisers. She remembers I ate them all as I tried to remain calm while she practiced driving.

They tease me about my use of the English language, when I said words like "lollygagging," and especially "goonballing." Lollygagging refers to wasting time. Goonballing may be an original word, describing the kids when they were goofing around and acting silly.

My role as a father to these three amazing people has brought me so much joy. I love them all and am deeply proud of Mari, Mike, and Ryan. Their faith, their kindness, their everyday efforts to try their best are evidence that some of the lessons my mom taught me have carried onward in our family…or maybe they did it on their own. Either way, I am very proud of them.

Chapter 8

End of an Era

I – Darkest Before Dawn

While both Martzie and I enjoyed our children, the two of us never quite found a comfortable space as a married couple. From my perspective, we always seemed to be fighting or getting over a fight. We talked about things but nothing much changed. I just figured we would keep going and maybe eventually, somehow we would find some peace.

Peace did not happen. Then Martzie's father died. Then she got breast cancer, which recurred a year later. It was a very difficult time in our lives. We tried Marriage Encounter and marriage counseling. We grew even further apart. I know I had a part in that separateness. I will also admit to making mistakes in my marriage that to this day I am not proud of. I deeply regret inflicting pain on Martzie and on our children.

While I was on a business trip in 1986, Martzie decided she had had enough and filed for divorce. I came back to find that I was no longer welcome in the family home. It was a shock. It crushed me not to live with my children and see them every day.

I signed a lease on a rather depressing apartment that was close to the family home, though by then Mari was already attending college and Mike was just about done with high school. Ryan, however, was still in grade school, and it was important to me to be able to see him and Mike and Mari as much as possible. Martzie and I tried to work things out, but after a year we agreed to divorce.

Those were dark days for me. Alone at night it felt like my world was ending. In a way it had. Everything I knew and felt proud of had been smashed to bits. I missed my kids. I felt uncomfortable at church because of the stigma attached to divorce. I didn't sleep well. Some nights I would just roll over and over in bed, worrying. I learned that my 4:00 a.m. thoughts could not be trusted. By that time of the night, my brain just coughed up evidence of my self-loathing, not workable solutions. I realized that I just had to hang on till morning. Some days I was a little surprised the sun still came up.

I remember stopping past the house one evening and Ryan came running down the driveway to greet me, waving a sheet of paper. He seemed excited and a little stressed.

Through the car window, he handed me the bracket of the Nebraska soapbox derby championship he had won the previous summer. There at the number one spot was his name. As a part of the winner's ceremony, they had given him the tournament bracket page. Ryan wanted me to have it—one of his most prized possessions. "Take it, Dad, I don't know when I'll ever see you again," he said. The broken pieces of my heart were so proud and simultaneously so sad. A few days later I took him to a park and played some catch. We didn't say much but it was good.

II - Lessons

There were a few things that helped me through those dark days: seeing the kids, visiting with some friends, church, prayer, long walks, and doing the very best job at work that I could. I learned that service to others can help raise your spirits in a way that nothing else can. I liked being able to help people, especially the less fortunate populations of Omaha who might not otherwise receive care.

Right before the separation, I got involved with a Creighton University service mission in the Dominican Republic (DR). I will talk much more about that mission later. What's important to mention here is that work gave me something to be proud of and to hope for. Every summer, I went there for a few weeks and would get lost in the work. Helping the Dominicans, working with the medical students who came with me, being a part of something much bigger reminded me that I did have value in the world. I couldn't fix my marriage, but I could still build something useful and important.

During my DR visit the summer after the separation, I had a chance to think. I realized that my role as a dad had changed. No longer the nightly homework guru, I couldn't just hover on the edges of their world. I needed more than a dim apartment to offer them. Previously, I had gotten a GMC van so I could chauffeur the kids to their activities, including soapbox derby races. Now I thought I should move to a house, with perhaps some water nearby so there was more to do at my house than sit on the couch.

Upon my return to Nebraska, I drove around each weekend looking at lakefront property. After a few weeks, I found a small home, half an hour south of Omaha along a string of small lakes...they called them lakes, anyway. The bodies of water actually used to be gravel pits, dug when the interstate was being constructed. In later years, the pits were filled up with water and a neighborhood developed around them. People could swim and float paddle boats, or walk the trail around them and enjoy the cottonwood trees. The new house was exactly what I had imagined in the DR. It was a place I could build a new life. I signed the papers, replaced the septic system, and moved in. About a month later, I was out for a walk. A neighborhood mother happened past with her baby, and I introduced myself.

"Hello. My name is Joe Lynch. I'm your new neighbor."

"Oh hello! It's nice to meet you. I know who you are; you just bought the pink house."

Huh? I thought to myself. When I got home, I called my son on the phone.

"Mike, is my new house pink?"

"Sure is, Dad."

"Oh," I said, and then paused. "What are you doing this summer?"

"I've got a house to paint," he replied. We both laughed. It seemed like it had been a long time since we had laughed spontaneously together. It felt good.

That summer Mike painted the house a nice earth-tone beige. Anyway, that's the color he told me it was.

Chapter 9

New Love

I - Terri

I wasn't thinking I would remarry. I had my kids, I had my work, and I had mission service that I enjoyed doing. What else did I need?

The answer, of course, was partnership. I didn't know it at the time, but there was a Terri-sized hole in my life.

For many years, I just worked and saw my kids. Eventually, though, I missed having someone to talk to, to be with, and to love. I started dating a bit. That's how I found myself at a Christmas dance in 1989. I spotted a pretty nurse I had seen a little at work and asked her to dance with me. Terri was so full of light and fun, I really liked her. We danced the entire night together. Then, I asked if I could take her home. She said yes, but before we were to leave, I went to the restroom. When I came out she was gone. I waited and waited for her, looking all over the building and out in the dark freezing parking lot. She wasn't anywhere. My Cinderella had apparently changed her mind.

We continued to pass one another in the halls at work, saying nothing about our evening of dancing. I wondered what had happened, sure, but figured she had decided she didn't actually like me after all. It seemed prudent not to pursue matters. Two years went by before Terri called me and invited me to *Madame Butterfly*. Sadly,

I was dating someone else at the time, a nurse in Harlan, Iowa, and had to decline.

More silence and another year passed. Meanwhile, the other woman and I broke up. Sometime later, trying to be a nice guy, I sent her some flowers as a sort of "No hard feelings" gesture. That would turn out to be a terrible idea.

Terri had been on my mind, and I thought, *maybe now. She called me. That must mean I have a chance with her.* So I phoned her and asked her to go bicycling one Saturday. Terri said she was unable to go that day. She was going to be traveling to Hawaii with some friends. I remember my spirits immediately deflated. I wasn't sure if that was true, or if she had decided she didn't want to date me. I was relieved when she suggested an alternative Saturday. *All right!* I thought. *Finally, a date with Terri!*

It probably sounds funny for a 49-year-old to have the same emotional turmoil around dating we expect from high-schoolers. The truth is, no matter how old you are, it never gets easier to make yourself vulnerable to rejection, especially if you really do like the other person. It's hard to be brave.

The day arrived for our bicycling adventure. It was sometime in August of 1991. I was supposed to meet Terri at 10:00. Of course, there was an emergency at work. I ended up being two hours late for our date. When I arrived, she seemed irritated. She sat me down across the living room from her. "Why are you here?" she asked.

"Well, I thought we were going to ride bikes..."

"Let me make one thing clear. I am not going to be your nurse in Omaha," she said.

"Huh?"

I had no idea what was happening. All that worry and anticipation to just ask her out and now I was undergoing an inquisition. I was flummoxed. Eventually, Terri explained the reason she was angry. She had done a little sleuthing after agreeing to go out with me. Through a friend in Harlan, she uncovered the flower delivery I had sent. She assumed that meant I had an ongoing relationship with another woman, and that I was collecting women across the region. I understood why she was cautious. Sometimes doctors do behave badly with nurses. But that wasn't what I was doing. I was just trying to be nice. I pleaded my case and asked her, "Please. Can we just have this first date?"

Eventually, we took that ride and had a great time. More fun and dating followed. We went to dinner, to plays, to church, to family events. I felt joyful about this new person in my life. Terri made me smile. She understood my work because she was immersed in the same field. And, completely independently of me, she had also committed to regular service at the Dominican mission. With all we have in common, it's funny that it took so long for us to connect. I am so glad that we kept trying. I love this woman. I love how her enthusiasm for life enlivens me. I love how her openness complements my quiet ways. Terri has made my life full.

I was fortunate to find her. I had known her as a colleague and friend. We shared goals and beliefs. Later, we were surprised and pleased to find out that her aunt and uncle and cousins knew some of my cousins and had attended mass together at St. Joseph's Catholic Church in Broken Bow, Nebraska, for many years.

II – Bigger Family

Not only did Terri increase my happiness, she increased my family size. After dating for a few months, Terri introduced me to her two children. Brenda, Terri's daughter, was attending Creighton as a philosophy undergraduate student. When she first came out to my house to meet me, I was nervous. I really wanted it to go well. I asked Terri what sort of things Brenda liked so we would have some things to talk about. Hearing that she spent a lot of time inside her head like I do, I chose four books as gifts, the most memorable one being *Angela's Ashes* by Frank McCourt. I love that book both for its Irishness and for McCourt's simple but stunning prose. Brenda revealed just how bookish she is too by immediately opening *Angela's Ashes* and reading parts. She couldn't wait to get into it. I was tickled by her reaction. We've been good friends ever since. She later told Terri that I was the best guy she had dated in a long time. It made me proud.

Terri's younger child is David. David was 18 when I started dating Terri. Because he has severe Down syndrome, meeting him was different than meeting Brenda. Instead of being worried about his assessment of me, I worried about Terri's reaction to my reaction to David. I wanted to get it right. What I discovered was how hard Terri has had to work in her life. David is not easy to care for. He doesn't speak or dress himself. He doesn't feed himself, and he can be grouchy. He communicates a few words through sign language, but other than that, it's hard to know what he wants or needs. Terri just seems to read his mind. Watching her love and care for David helped me see what a kind and patient woman she is. Lifelong care for a handicapped adult is a huge commitment. When I grasped the enormity of that, my admiration for Terri grew exponentially.

Terri and I started dating in August of 1991. It didn't take long before we started thinking about getting married. The fit was so great, it seemed natural. We worried, though, that the courtship was too short. Things seemed to be clicking along so easily, it was eerie in some ways. Both of us had experienced divorce, and neither of us wanted to ever feel that pain again. We were concerned enough about that to seek out a therapist. When we met with her we explained our concern. "There must be something wrong here because, you know, this is going too well."

She said, "You know, it doesn't hurt to go a little fast. This new person in your life isn't really new. You have known of each other, and worked with each other for ten years. You know their friends. You know their reputation...you know who they are. That's different than if you just met them in a bar last week."

That made us feel better about the pace. We recognized that unlimited time was not a given in life, and we had both found a special partner. Terri and I married in May of 1992 in Coeur d'Alene, Idaho. She moved into the lake house, and we merged our two families. We began a tradition of referring to our collective children as "our children," not "yours or mine." We try to offer all our kids the same love and support.

Mari had just finished college and was married, Mike and Brenda were in college, and Ryan was in high school when we were married. Ryan still lived with his mother, though I got to see him often on our drives to school. David came to stay with Terri and me, on alternate weeks at first. Later, he lived with us full time. Brenda, David, Mari, Mike, and Ryan are all special and important in our family. It has been a privilege to be able to watch them become adults.

On our first anniversary, I realized I wasn't happy with the ring I had given Terri at our wedding. It was such a busy time, we were in a hurry to get everything pulled together in time for the ceremony, and we had decided on matching gold bands. Now was the time to give her a proper ring. I went back to the jeweler where we first shopped for rings. The one she had loved and then decided she could never accept was still there. Terri had declaimed at the time that it was too expensive, but I decided I wanted her to have it.

It's not easy for me to make romantic gestures; they're not really in my vocabulary. I want to be that sort of person, but I don't always think of it. Or when I do, I'm a little uncomfortable about it. And, because of the color issues, sometimes, I have a hard time picking out presents. Flowers, I can do. Any kind of jewelry or clothing is hard. Because many colors are considered gendered and people tell me that certain combinations just don't go together, I can never be sure that something I pick isn't ridiculous. But I already knew that Terri loved this ring, so I was confident that she would be happy about it.

I booked a reservation at a nice restaurant. Over dinner, I took the ring out of my jacket pocket and said, "It's time for a ring." I gave it to her. Terri didn't look happy at all about this surprise. She said, "Oh, no. You shouldn't have done that. It cost way too much." Then she stood up and started heading for the bathroom while saying, "Take it back!" She marched off to the ladies' room, leaving the entire restaurant looking at me thinking *My, that didn't work.*

Five minutes later, Terri came back, pulled up her chair, sat down, looked at me and said, "Try again, I'm better now." *Phew,* I thought, and then smiled. She is a funny woman, and I appreciate her ability to regroup.

My family was happy for me to have someone. Terri treated me with affection and took to my children naturally. Two years after we were married, my sister, Pat, said out of the blue, "Joe, you really got lucky. Really lucky." Her tone indicated that she hadn't held out great hopes for my love life. I think Pat was right. I did get lucky when I connected with Terri. I am a lucky man indeed.

Terri has made my life much richer than it was. In many ways, Terri helps interpret the world for me. She helps me understand the social subtext. She plans the celebrations and invites all the kids. (She plans my outfits too.) Together, we have developed a bond of trust, love, and respect that enriches my life every day. Because of her I have love, fun, and friends. With her on my arm, I am included in her much broader social world. We investigate new places and things all the time. If it were just me, I would literally be going in the same circle all the time. Home, work, grocery, home... But Terri can't bear the monotony, so I have to challenge myself to keep up with her. We try new restaurants; we go to plays; we have parties. Every day is a new adventure. She keeps me young.

III - Brenda

Getting to know Brenda a little better was fun for me. I like to think that perhaps I have been a positive influence on her, just as she has been on me. Before I married her mother, I remember giving Brenda a hard time while watching her study for a philosophy test. She was preparing for a semester exam by flipping through the textbook the night before. I gathered that she had skipped quite a few of the class sessions. I had two reactions. I totally identified with being smart enough to coast a bit, and because of that, not knowing what to work on when it came time for the test. At the same time, the medical schoolteacher in me was appalled.

"Isn't there a study sheet?"

Brenda looked up and shrugged. "I don't know." She checked, and there was a five-page study guide.

"That study sheet is a contract between you and the teacher," I said. "You don't flip through the whole damn book the night before the test. You fill out the sheet. With that guide, the teacher is telling you what's important to study. If you know everything in those study sheets, you're guaranteed to pass the test. I don't know if you'll get an A, but you will pass the test."

Brenda trusted me, worked with the study guide, and got an A. She seemed to like me a little more after that. Helping Brenda along in her education and career has been fulfilling.

Just like Terri has, I think I've had some influence on our family culture too. Like the time Brenda was trying to decide where to go to graduate school for law. Because her pre-law exam results were so good, Brenda was accepted at several prestigious law schools around the country. Checking with Terri and me, she said, "Is that okay?" *Uhhh...* I thought. With four kids all in college at the same time (Mari was now taking postgraduate classes), we weren't really able to swing Ivy League type tuition. I proposed that we provide what it would cost to attend University of Nebraska law school. Brenda would be welcome to use that at any of her top schools, but would have to cover the rest of the cost herself. She opted for U of N. Smart choice, I thought.

Based on Brenda's career path, U of N worked out just fine. She has been clerking for the Nebraska Supreme Court for fifteen years. They trust her to write the briefs on cases that come before the court, which means that the information she gathers and interprets is the basis for the biggest legal arguments in the state. Clearly, I am proud of her.

In her personal life, Brenda reminds me of Terri. That makes me smile. She's a free spirit, constantly thinking of new places to go explore and have adventures with her kids and her husband. To her, not having been somewhere is a plus. For me, that's a negative. If I'm along for the fun, our discussion often goes like this:

Me: "Why would I go there when there's another place that I know I like?"

Brenda: "Well, we haven't seen what's over there, and somebody told me it was good. Why not?"

She's usually right. Adventures with her are fun.

IV – David

My mom set an example of kindness and respect for all types of people. As an adult, I have tried hard to practice that philosophy in my work and personal life. I try to be compassionate, and I encouraged that in the students I taught as well. When I met David, that level of compassion wasn't enough. It was surface-level kindness. I had to go deeper, love harder, to come to terms with David's levels of need.

When a difficult patient comes under my care, I do all I can to help him. But then I get to go home and rest. With David, that's not possible. That probably sounds selfish. I don't mean it to. David's needs are those of a two- or three-year-old. He needs help with every single thing. If he doesn't want to do something, he resists just like a toddler does. When parents encounter that in an actual toddler, they can be patient—in part—because they know that one day the behavior will pass. What David has now is all the maturity he's ever going to have. Sometimes that reality is tiring and frustrating. Terri describes David as a double-edged sword, one of our greatest joys and greatest sorrows. However, she often repeats the expression that he is our "angel child." And he is...most of the time.

That being said, there are upsides to being David's "Daddy Joe." I was pleased the first time I was able to teach David something. When he first came to us, he used to hit a lot. One day he hit us. Terri, David, and I had a long conversation about our house rules.

"We don't hit, and you don't hit. We don't hit at our house."

He's never hit again. Then, I offered a substitution. "You can wave your arm if you feel angry." So, he does that a lot now, which makes me proud. He learned to adapt to a new situation and he listened to me. Sometimes David will lean toward me, which is his way of showing love. An established non-hugger, I like that kind of affection. David is my kind of hugger.

Out in public, I can get a little frustrated with people who completely ignore him as if he is invisible. We do appreciate the kindness and the generous remarks that people occasionally say to us. Mostly, now, I have come to understand that most people are just not sure what to say or do about David. Sometimes I think that TV actors with Down syndrome project a rosy picture that doesn't accurately represent the full spectrum of the disorder. Yes, there are high-functioning kids and adults with Down's. And it's true that they are often joyful. There are also low-functioning people, and that's where David is. In the U.S., we gloss over the hard stuff in favor of the ideal.

However, in the Dominican Republic, the experience is different. When we take David there, residents revere him, not patronize him. The first time we experienced that, I was taken by surprise. But I came to understand that many Dominicans think of those with Down syndrome as angel people. One day, David and I were walking through a smaller town in the DR. A woman came running up to us with a baby, all wrapped in fine gowns. She placed that baby right in David's hands before I could warn her not to. I silently willed David, *Don't drop it! Don't drop it!* He didn't drop the baby. He did smile. I learned that it's considered a blessing of sorts for an angel person to hold your baby. Who knows? Maybe it is a blessing. It was certainly a special moment.

As I said, the Dominican culture views David differently than Americans do. Witnessing that has helped me to view my son differently too. Dominicans move aside on the bus to make way for David. They come right up and hug or kiss him. They talk to him normally. "Hola, David. ¿Cómo estás?" David doesn't speak Spanish, but he doesn't speak English either. He does, however, know what people's intentions are when they address him. He knows the difference between kindness and derision.

Terri and I were very worried about bringing David with us the first time we attempted to all go together. Would he be safe? Would he find the new situation overwhelming? What would he eat? Would he do okay without his favorite TV shows? Those worries were unfounded. David actually thrives in the Dominican Republic. The mission where we stay is small enough that David can find his way around easily. He loves to dance to the Dominican music, especially merengue. He would dance and dance for as long as we kept the music going with all kinds of people during our "fiestas." He danced with Terri, students, and Dominicans, sweating and smiling for hours. Mostly, the food at the mission is rice and beans, and fresh fruits and vegetables, which he loves.

Sometimes, we Americans look condescendingly at countries like the DR. We see the lack of iPads or convenience food in the *campos* and mistake that for poor quality of life. If David could talk, he would tell you it's better there. Kindness is easier to find, spirituality lives comfortably within daily life, there's a lot of love to be found in the Dominican Republic. David understood their language, the language of love.

Chapter 10

Mission Work in the Dominican Republic

I – Why

Up to this point in the book, I have mentioned my mission work in the Dominican Republic in passing. I don't want this book to be a preachy tome; however this part of my life is extremely important. I want to take this chapter to explain why that is true.

Growing up, most kids lean on the faith of their parents. They go to church because they are taken there. They pray because that's what the family is doing. This model was true for me too until I became a young adult. Somewhere between watching my mother build an independent life with the church as her foundation, and visiting the Amazon mission with Father Krupski, my own seedling of faith bloomed. I began to see just how sustaining it is to have a life of faith, humility, and service.

That strength comes directly from Jesus's example. He valued love, kindness, compassion and mercy. I try to do the same. My experiences as a child, in my career, in service, and throughout my travels have primarily been with what I would call "the gentle people" of the world. That is my world. That is my church. As Pope Francis says, "A church without charity does not exist."

Somehow, the challenge to live a life of compassion and faith is easier in the DR. God seems closer there. Though the circumstances are often heartbreaking, the question is often simple. Can we help? If the answer is yes in any form, then we do. For example, one summer a stranger arrived at the mission gates, asking for us. This skinny, sickly Dominican man could hardly stand, yet he had ridden on the back of a motorcycle to get to us. He said a friend of ours had mentioned that we might help him. I listened to his story of having active AIDS, experiencing rejection and lack of care in his community. He had nowhere to go. He was hungry, thirsty, tired, in pain, and had only the clothes on his back. He rested and told his story of misery.

We listened and Terri began to gather food, water, medicine, and clothing for him. David's elastic-waist sweatpants were perfect for him! The kitchen willingly boxed up food for him. Clean water is plentiful at the mission. The man rested and we opened our arms as wide as possible, allowing him to feel that a loving heart was there for him. It was easy for us to provide these basic necessities that day, but what about the next day? Or the one after that? One lesson I have had to learn over and over is to just live in the moment and do what I can right then. We wondered where he would go. He said if we could spare a few pesos, he would get another motorcycle ride to a friend's house. Off he went, holding tightly to the driver of the motorcycle.

Was this an example of the living Word of Christ? Perhaps. Are we able to recognize Christ in the poor, the sick, and the marginalized? Not always, but on this day I felt we had risen to the challenge that was presented to us. We did the best we could.

For me, mission work is an extension of my faith. The Church *is* the people, and those are *my* people. The people in the field and all those who support them, in the slums, in the food lines, on the Pine Ridge Indian Reservation, in the Dominican Republic and in Haiti, building a brick factory in the Amazon, the seminarians singing their prayers so beautifully in Tanzania, the people working at the Siena Francis House for the homeless in Omaha...their work is built on the gospel. I love those people. They are the Church. I love their work, and I love our Church with a deep-seated passion.

I have returned to the Dominican Republic for 30 years now because this work gives me the opportunity to renew my faith, to teach my students the same lesson, and to be of service to the people there. Though I think I get more in return than I give.

II - What

I have explained my motives behind my mission work, but not really what my work in the Dominican Republic actually entails. The mission in the DR is affiliated with a Creighton University program, the Institute for Latin American Concern or ILAC. Physically, it consists of an office at Creighton University with three employees, and a five-acre campus in the Dominican Republic with 35 or so employees, all Dominicans. Creighton University helped started the program, but does not own the five-acre campus in the Dominican Republic. That's a separate, faith-based Dominican NGO. Outside that main campus are 150 or so campos, or villages, that the students travel to during their stay.

I think the key to our longevity in the DR is the grassroots buy-in from community members there. Our work not only serves residents, we employ residents because the only way to be of legitimate service is to know what the people need and want. These residents are the real anchor of the ILAC program. In each campo, there is a local person or two who is chosen by the villagers, called *cooperadoras*. They receive first aid training from ILAC. Then, they go back and they live and help in the community. That person is the one who invites us to come to their villages. We only serve communities where we have been invited.

Another very important piece of ILAC is the exchange of gifts. Our participants are there to learn from the Dominicans just as much as we are there to teach. So, unlike some mission programs around the world, we aren't primarily trying to preach to the locals. Mostly, they are already Catholic; they don't need evangelizing. Plus, they are holier and more faithful than most of us are.

Every summer, Creighton recruits and sends groups of students, with faculty, to the ILAC center in Santiago. There are many different programs involving healthcare and other teams. There are nursing, medical, dental, pharmacy, undergraduate and many other students and professionals. Occupational Therapy, Physical Therapy and other college and high school programs also participate. There is an extensive water quality program for the campos, directed by the Creighton chemistry department. There is also a Creighton Law School program as well as a semester-long program for undergraduate students. Brenda was part of the first undergraduate semester-abroad program in 1992 in Santiago. Our goal in bringing students to the region is to help them discover how much they can learn from the villagers. By the end, most students have gained a new respect for the Dominicans' faithfulness and diversity.

ILAC began 10 years before I got involved. About 40 years ago, two young Jesuits, Ernesto Travieso and Narciso Sanchez, who were originally from Cuba, began the program while they were studying in Toronto. They built this program around three values: service, immersion, and spirituality or thoughtfulness. (I like the word thoughtfulness more than spirituality, but they're the same thing to me.) Over a period of years, the mission combined with Creighton University. Father Travieso became chaplain of the medical school, establishing Terri's and my main volunteer work, called The Summer Program. As medical director of this mission, my primary role was helping to recruit the medical students and professionals, and supervising the effort to ensure the work was happening as it should. Over the years, the program has evolved so that it runs fairly smoothly. It wasn't always that way.

III – My Early Days in the DR

I remember the first year I went to the DR. It was 1985 and I was excited to see what this new program was about. ILAC rented St Pio X Seminary in Licey, a small community on the edge of Santiago. I was assigned to the campo of Arroyo Del Toro. In those days, there were no real roads to the campos. We would ride in jeeps, vans and pickup trucks until the road ended and the path to the campo began. There was a group of Dominicans waiting for us with their burros. We carried our personal and medical supplies (enough for one month) for the clinic on our backs. Clinic medicine, materials, supplies, equipment, and food were carefully packed by the Dominicans on their burros. We loaded our backpacks to trek up the mountain. It was a brutal hike, lasting over two hours.

At the campo, we were led to our new homes and met our Dominican hosts. We dropped off our backpacks and went to set up our clinics, usually in an empty schoolhouse. We used sheets and clothespins and ropes to divide the space into exam rooms and a pharmacy. We arranged the waiting area and exam areas and the pharmacy. The dentists set up outside so they had better light to see. They used rocking chairs tipped back and secured for their patients. Since they were outside, they set up rope lines to keep the crowd back and not have so many spectators.

In my campo home, I tried to talk to my hosts. We called them our parents, no matter our age. My Spanish has always been limited, but they laughed and encouraged me. Rural Dominican Spanish is a world/language of its own, with no s's and limited conjugation of verbs. "Trabajai" for" trabajar" and "como esta usted" often becomes "ta."

Campo life contrasted wildly with life in Omaha. The children grabbed our hands and pulled us around. The men played dominos with sounds of jovial chatter interspersed with a loud bang each time they slammed a domino down. The dogs were tied up, while the chickens wandered about. Occasional massive pigs slept in their pens. In our Dominican campo home, we assembled army style cots that we had brought and put them on the dirt floor. My roommate was John Marley, an older, saintly dentist and Creighton University faculty member who had already been to the DR a half-dozen times.

The roosters crowed all night and all day, so morning was instead announced by the family prayer time. We awoke to the mother saying the rosary softly with the father and children doing the response in a sleepy tone. Then the fire was lit outside and "Radio Santa Maria" was turned on to news and church music. In those days, there was no running water or electricity to the villages but battery power was available to most of them.

John and I dressed and brushed our teeth in front of the children intentionally, as good examples. As we headed out the door to go where our group was to eat breakfast, the mother stopped us. "Café?" She handed us a small cup of very strong coffee. "Azucar?" (sugar?) as she put the first spoonful in my cup. "No quiero mas azucar." (I don't care for more sugar). We would stop and sip the coffee, thank her and tell her we needed to be on our way as she tried to give us more.

At breakfast and all the meals, we ate as a group, sitting around a table after saying or singing grace. We could see dozens of people gathering at our makeshift clinic. Our local Dominican organizer would hand out numbered tickets, guaranteeing that they would be seen in the medical or dental clinic that day. Later, in the afternoons we would rest or visit homes in the area. In the evenings we had reflection meetings a few nights a week. These were a relaxed combination of reflection, sharing, and prayer. Organizational type meetings were separate.

We called this particular community the singing campo. One of our American female students had a spectacular voice, as did one of our Dominican ILAC seminarian helpers. There were also a remarkable number of Dominican *campesinos* with wonderful voices. Years later, our Dominican helper married a Creighton medical student. They and their five beautiful children live in Omaha and we have remained friends.

One night, our Dominican mother served John and me limoncea tea (like hot lemon tea). I loved it and told them so. Unfortunately, whenever I drank it in the evening, I had to urinate at night and it was a project to get to the outhouse because they often locked up the house at night. I tried to stop them, but, in their typical generosity, they served it to me every night anyway. They even gave me a group of limoncea plants for me to take home to the states, which is quite illegal, but I couldn't bring myself to tell them and accepted the plants graciously.

One evening, John Marley, our dentist, said that our group's American coordinator, a recent college graduate and rather intense dedicated young man who later became a Jesuit scholastic, had told him the lines for the dental clinic were too long. He thought John should only pull one tooth, and do no more with each patient in order to speed things up. John asked me what I thought he should do. I offered the solution I had seen work best in situations like these. "Just smile and say okay, and keep doing the same thing you have been doing all along." He laughed and said okay, and continued treating his patients his way.

Interactions with colleagues and residents were often tricky since we didn't know each other well and multiple cultures crossed paths through this mission work. That was the case the time I hiked to Agua de Juan with two American Jesuit scholastics and a young Dominican. Excited to be out on a beautiful day doing work we believed in, the scholastics and I set a brisk pace up the steep hill, leaving behind the Dominican who was carrying a very heavy backpack. Soon, I recognized our mistake; the hike up the hill toward Agua de Juan was the steepest I had ever experienced. It is almost impossible to describe how steep it was. I thought I was going to die, but onward we trekked. The scholastics never rested. I didn't want to slow them down, so didn't say anything about needing a break. The tortoise to us hares, the Dominican slowly, methodically passed us all. When we eventually arrived, completely exhausted, a campesino woman looked at my face and exclaimed loudly, "Colorado!" (Red!) Again, my Irish complexion announced itself.

Later, the scholastics and I sat together and talked about the journey. We realized that we all had really wanted to take a break when climbing the hill. Embarrassed that an older man was seemingly energetic, they kept grinding upward though a rest would have been better for all of us. We obviously needed to communicate better.

IV - Students

The students who volunteer for these trips are already really special people. We recognize that anyone who has signed up to offer service like this has already demonstrated passion for effecting change in the world. We merely guide them to pay attention to the gifts the Dominicans are offering in return.

"Blessed are the meek; for they shall inherit the earth," Mathew 5:5 tells us. To me, Dominican "meekness" looks like serenity and joy. Despite hardship and sickness, these gentle people appear to be at peace with themselves. Contrast that with a Western perspective. We Americans have so much material wealth, yet we seem unhappy much of the time. When my students discover this disparity between cultural contentedness, they are always surprised.

When Creighton students sign up to volunteer in a developing country, we ask them why. Students often say, "I want to go to help." By the time they have finished with their service program, they are often transformed by the love and generosity they experience with the rural Dominicans, who are warm and gentle, and prayerful. They usually say, at the end, that they received far more than they gave. Then we ask, "Were you changed in any way?" It is often apparent that they have had a change in heart...an understanding of what it is to live, even for a short period of time, in solidarity with the poor. Sometimes they even suffer a little. In experiencing that, however small, they understand how much of the world lives.

That's why I really do this work. I like seeing that shift in thinking. I like it when the light bulbs turn on. I like affirming the idea that individuals actually can make a difference in the world. Life has a way of banging those idealistic dreams out of us. I'm trying to help students see that there are opportunities to learn and to be of service all through life. I want them to hold on to that passion to be of service. And I want to remind myself of that as well.

One particularly memorable light bulb was that of my own daughter, Mari, finding a way to offer comfort. In 1989, Mari was a junior at Creighton. She joined in on the mission trip that summer and went to Agua de Juan near the Haitian border. One day, she didn't feel well so she stayed in the campo clinic while the rest of the group went out. While everyone was gone, a mother brought a sick child to the clinic. Mari was alone and the clinic was closed. Mari said she didn't know what to do. She didn't have any medical knowledge. She was just serving as an ayudante, or helper, in the clinic. So she just took the child in her arms and held her, rocking and talking softly for a few hours until the medical team returned. As the group returned, one clinician saw her and took a picture through the open window as she held the now sleeping child. (See photo in center section.) The grace and compassion Mari embodied that day still makes me stop in awe whenever I look at the photograph. That moment sums up our entire Dominican experience. Many of the problems are so big, no one person can fix them entirely, but each of us can do something to help one other person.

During the summer that Mari was with me, my sons Ryan and Mike also came to the DR. They were ages 13 and 18 then. We three traveled around the countryside, meeting up with Mari and her group in Samana. I was so happy to be able to include my children in my mission work. It made me so proud of them to see how they engaged people and adapted to the challenges of life there. Coincidentally, Terri happened to be on the same plane as the boys, coming to volunteer her nursing skills for the second session that summer. She and I only knew each other professionally at that time. I consider it a beautiful twist of fate that Terri met the boys on the plane. She also met Mari because they were assigned to neighboring campos, and the groups visited each other during the program. I'm sure it didn't occur to her during those encounters that one day she would date and marry their father. Maybe there are no coincidences, but only "God-incidents."

Each time Terri and I serve in the DR, we are changed in ways we don't even begin to understand until later. Each year, it is a journey of formation and spiritual renewal. Each time there is an "ah-ha" moment, a lesson learned; there is a personal encounter with Christ. We are called to love and serve, to be in community and be present to others. When we see that there are injustices and oppression and poverty, we try to work together with the Dominicans to problem solve, to offer a hand up, not a hand out, to teach them to fish, not just give them a fish. The Jesuits call this "faith that does justice."

Sometimes when I'm there, the action and intensity are overwhelming. Sometimes there is peace and a quiet love that fills the heart. It is easy for me to be intellectual. I am often "in my head," as they say. It can be a long way between my head and my heart. Somehow when I work in the DR, I am broken open. My heart breaks from witnessing real human suffering, and sometimes my heart is filled with peace and joy. It is hard to explain, and I don't want to sound "preachy." I am inept in explaining feelings and what draws me back to the ILAC programs in the Dominican Republic.

Perhaps this will help. This is a segment of an article Terri wrote for the Jesuit magazine, *Company,* winter 2003-04 issue, titled, "From the Heart":

> Creighton teams go on tours, activities, and field trips away from the clinics where they work to learn about Dominican culture. One weekend in spring 2002, we took seventeen physical therapy students to Crossroads, a mission near Puerto Plata run by Jana and Bob, an American couple. Jana had invited us to join them in one of their many ministries to the poor, serving lunch to Haitians who live in a garbage dump.
>
> But first she talked about dignity and respect. She told the students not to hold their noses because, yes, it will really smell bad, but you will be in their home. She said not to make faces of shock, of horror. All they have is their dignity. Please don't take it away

from them. They will want to sing for you to honor and thank you, and they would like it if you sing for them.

So off we went on roads that dump trucks traveled and then on paths meandering through piles of trash. The Haitians gathered around us with drums made of old rusty five-gallon cooking oil cans. Broken metal spoons served as drumsticks. Other unrecognizable objects suddenly became musical instruments. They sang a traditional Haitian song, a joyful sound in a most dismal environment.

We came prepared when it was our turn to sing. One student, John, pulled out his shiny guitar, and we sang, *"How Great Thou Art."* For a moment we entered a sacred space in another culture, with another people living in the most horrendous conditions, and connected and exchanged gifts of our humanity through song.

V - Sharing Gifts

Again and again, the Dominicans show me what it is to be truly filled with faith. Like on Good Friday morning in 2002, we were awakened by the most beautiful song I have ever heard, *"Tengo un Nuevo Amor, Jesus,"* which translates to *"I have a new love, Jesus."* A recording of the song was being broadcast throughout the neighborhood on a loudspeaker. It was the first time we had ever heard the song. We went outside of our casita and sat on the little porch, listening to the music in the early morning darkness. It was a special moment for us. It was difficult to understand the words in Spanish, but we could feel the passion and love filling the neighborhood. Then on Easter Sunday, Henry, a local musician, sang that same song at mass at the ILAC Mission church. I did not completely understand all the words, but the spirit and the music in the church were overpowering. Terri told him then how much she loved that song. Now when we return to mass at the ILAC church, Henry frequently plays this song… maybe because Terri loves it so and is moved to tears.

People in my world often say, "The Word is still relevant." They mean that the words of Jesus, the gospels, are still alive and important. We experience the truth of this message every time we work in the DR. Especially when events slow down and I can listen, this gospel comes to mind.

Matthew 25:34-40 (New American Standard Bible)
34 "Then the King will say to those on His right, 'Come, you who are blessed of My Father, inherit the kingdom prepared for you from the foundation of the world. 35 For I was hungry, and you gave Me something to eat; I was thirsty, and you gave Me something to drink; I was a stranger, and you invited Me in; 36 naked, and you clothed Me; I was sick, and you visited Me; I was in prison, and you came to Me.' 37 Then the righteous will answer Him, 'Lord, when did we see You hungry, and feed You, or thirsty, and give You something to drink? 38 And when did we see You a stranger, and invite You in, or naked, and clothe You? 39 When did we see You sick, or in prison, and come to You?' 40 The King will answer and say to them, 'Truly I say to you, to the extent that you did it to one of these brothers of Mine, even the least of them, you did it to Me.'"

Talking about my service makes me a little uncomfortable. I don't want to be self-congratulatory, and I truly feel like I gain more than I give. However, I share these stories—these gifts I have been given—because I want my community and my family to understand why I have devoted so much of my life to this mission.

Not every gift has fancy wrapping paper or prompts a thank-you in response. Nonetheless, these reminders of humility and gratitude are gifts. For example, consider my experiences in the Dominican *bateyes*. Bateyes are common in the Dominican Republic and consist of groups of Haitians who live in permanent camps of sorts. The communities usually began as groups of Haitians who obtained contracts to work and live temporarily in the DR, mostly working in the sugarcane fields. Over the years, communities often remained, even as the Dominican sugarcane industry became less profitable and jobs became scarce. Today there are generations of Haitians living in bateyes, some legal, most probably not. Many of them have never been to Haiti and know nothing about it, but they do not have Dominican birth certificates and are not approved by the government of the DR to attend school or work legally. Fortunately, many of the Dominican teachers ignore the rules and accept the undocumented children into their schools. The Haitians living in the bateyes are truly a people without a country. They are without documents or rights in any country. Their living conditions are far more impoverished than the Dominicans'.

Father Don Doll, SJ related this batey story that has stuck with me. Father Doll was talking with a Haitian who offered him some of the soup he was cooking. The soup looked to be a pot of water cooked into broth with a few bones. Father Doll appreciated the gesture, but wasn't hungry and said so. "No, no tengo hambre. No, pero gracias." (No, I am not hungry but thank you.) The gentleman said, "Siempre hambre." (I am always hungry.)

It is hard to grasp that kind of hunger. That level of poverty when there is not enough to eat, every day, always. And yet, he offered to share.

The first time I went to Batey Libertad, I was told we were going for a "thank you" performance put on by the Haitian community who lived there. Before my visit, the ILAC Center had asked the leaders of this batey, how can we help you? What is it, as a community, you would like? We thought they would ask for more latrines, to clean the nearby stream so they could have clean water, or more healthcare, or maybe a few jobs. Instead, they asked if we could help them build a community center, somewhere they could all meet together.

So, ILAC helped them build it. It was more of a large open-air gazebo with an elevated concrete floor and open walls. When we arrived that day for the performance, we all talked for a while. I met a thin elderly Haitian man who, I was told, had been the local schoolteacher. The school had been closed for some time, and he worked in town now. Still, each evening, he spent a few hours teaching with anyone who wished to attend. I asked him, who pays you to teach now? He said no one. I asked him, why do you keep doing it? He paused, and then said, "Because I am their teacher." I felt humbled and slightly idiotic for asking.

Later, after a small snack of crackers and cheese, a group of young Haitian dancers gathered and began singing, then dancing, and more dancing. How they danced! Wild, beautiful, with wonderful rhythms, on and on they danced. Finally they were done. We stood and applauded and hugged them.

That night, after I was back at the ILAC Center, I asked myself: *Why do they dance?* That question has recurred in my mind many more times since that day. As I sit in my living room in Omaha, with heat and cool air as needed, with carpet on the floor and plenty of food in the kitchen, it's hard not to wonder what they have to be happy about. Every trip to this special island reminds me that those material things really aren't the path to happiness. Perhaps the answer to "why do they dance" is much like the teacher's response to my question. Perhaps they dance because they are human.

VI - ILAC duties

Since 1986, I have volunteered in the DR for varying lengths of time. Even now, at 75, I'm still at it, though I'm cutting down. Likewise, Terri was involved in volunteering starting in 1989. Until we married, we weren't ever in the same area at the same time, though this shared mission was one more element that strengthened our relationship from the start. Initially, our summer visits to the DR were in two-week blocks. Later, they would become seven or eight weeks in length, from the time we arrived in Santiago to begin preparations for the summer program, until it ended with the beautiful sunset mass with the students on the beach, in Sosua.

Over the years, both of us have been assigned to ILAC roles that we did not feel adequately prepared for. I once served as interim Executive Director of the ILAC Mission in Santiago. I served on the Board of Directors and as the Health Care/Medical Director of Creighton ILAC programs. Terri served as the ILAC Director of the Creighton University office. We didn't apply for any of these positions, nor did we feel like we were qualified to do the jobs. But we trusted the people around us, both at Creighton University and in the Dominican Republic.

One man in particular was a trusted resource and advisor as I tried to navigate a leadership role with ILAC. At the beginning of 2002, I had been appointed the interim Executive Director of the Dominican arm of ILAC. Alvaro Quesada was President of the ILAC board at the time. I considered him a good friend. I admired his skill at business and his devotion to family.

When I was brought in, I had been told this would be easy. I wouldn't have to hire or fire anyone. Just keep things running. I soon discovered that wasn't true. Things were in some disarray, and it was my job to stabilize things at the Center and to also help find my replacement, a permanent Executive Director. And then came the question of what to do with the present operational manager. For his privacy, I'll just call him Mateo, though that isn't his name. The board members, including Alvaro, asked me to decide whether to keep Mateo or let him go. Alvaro said he would help, and set up regular Friday meetings for us to keep in touch.

I wasn't sure about Mateo. The Dominicans seemed to like him, but something seemed off to me. I lay awake every night for three months trying to decide what to do about him. In addition to personnel matters, I was in charge of the organizational budget. One Friday, I asked Alvaro to look over my draft of the next annual budget. Money was pretty tight; it's always pretty tight, actually.

I asked Alvaro, "Who gets a raise?"

He said, "Don't worry, no raises. None! The way things are going in the country, they will be happy they still have a job."

I relayed that message to Mateo, the manager, but when he submitted the final budget, he had given himself and the accountant large raises. He had also given one person a pay cut, Jose Miguel. Unfortunately for Mateo, Jose Miguel was the one employee I knew well from my experience with him through the years. I knew he was superb, the heart of the ILAC program in Santiago. There was no way his performance warranted a pay cut. This didn't make sense to me. Something uncomfortable was happening here. I went to Alvaro and told him about the raises and the pay cut, and that I had some other problems with the manager. Something needed to be done about Mateo.

Alvaro said, "I agree with you. Obviously, you have to fire him."

I said, "Uhhh, okay. How do you fire someone in the DR?"

"Oh, it's easy. You just put a letter that says he is fired in an envelope. Give it to him on Friday afternoon."

"Shouldn't I talk to him?" I asked.

Alvaro replied, "No. It is not necessary and probably not a good idea."

So, on Friday, I gave Mateo the letter. The following Monday morning, before I told the employees that he had been fired, Mateo arrived at work and announced that he was calling a meeting of all employees.

Oh no, I thought. *Maybe I should have talked to him.* I asked Mateo if we could meet and he said okay. Since my Spanish wasn't very good and his English wasn't any better, we found a Peace Corps volunteer, a trusted friend of his, to act as a translator since the subject was obviously sensitive.

I relayed the message to him. "It won't work between you and ILAC—it just won't. It is just a matter of time. We are too different, etc." This meeting went on for two hours. At first, Mateo was clearly very angry and ready to cause problems. Slowly, he calmed down. He seemed to be absorbing what I was saying. When we were both exhausted, Mateo suddenly stood up, said, "You are a good man," shook my hand and left. He visited the ILAC Center once in a while after that but never caused any trouble.

Shortly after that situation with Mateo, we had a local ILAC board meeting. At its conclusion, Alvaro said he was flying to Port-au-Prince, Haiti, the next day for an important business meeting. He said he was a little concerned about the weather. One of the board members said, "You will be okay as long as you use the same plane and the same pilot you always use." The next day, for some reason the plane was not available. When he obtained another plane, it required a different pilot. They flew to Port-au-Prince, but were unable to land because of bad weather. They turned back to return to Santiago, but on the way back their plane disappeared.

We were in Boca Chica when we got the news. Soon, the plane's wreckage was spotted high in the mountains. Rescuers were attempting to reach the plane to see if there were any survivors. The search and rescue mission was very closely followed by the entire nation on radio and TV, since Alvaro was a well-known businessman. It took two days for them to reach the wreckage.

I remember walking to the Quesada home to join a group trying to comfort Alvaro's wife and wait for news. Joining me in the walk was Daniel Hendrickson, a member of the Creighton University faculty and a Jesuit who was assigned to ILAC to teach that semester. We were almost to the home when we heard a cell phone ring near us. After a short conversation, we overheard, "Todos son muertos." Alvaro, Alvarito, his only son, and the pilot were all dead. I can still hear those words. We all miss Alvaro, even now.

Throughout the turmoil of firing Mateo and Alvaro's death, there was still an employee search going on. Before his death, Alvaro had begun organizing plans to hire a Dominican for the job of Executive Director. We all thought that the program in Santiago would be more likely to be successful if it was led by a Dominican. He recommended advertising in *Listin Diario*, the nation's largest newspaper, based in Santo Domingo. After selecting a pool of applicants, a committee of four, including Terri and I, planned to interview the candidates.

We placed an ad in English in the newspaper. We received 75 applicants from whom we selected 25 to consider. The interviews were conducted in English so we could evaluate their English language skills. We assumed they were fluent in Spanish. We met very talented, pleasant, interesting people, most of whom had no concept of our mission and vision. There were physicians, writers, former newspaper editors, academicians, wealthy people who lived in Santo Domingo who thought they would commute to Santiago, and many others.

These interviews were done slowly over the course of several months. Alvaro's death slowed the process down. We were down to a very few applicants when we met Radalme Pena. He had a degree in business from the Pontificia Universidad Católica Madre y Maestra (Pontifical Catholic University of Mary, Mother and Teacher) in Santiago. He also had managed a free zone and had worked in New York. He presently managed his father's farm near Santiago, returning to farming after finding New York unsatisfying. We asked him, "Why are you interested in this job?" He replied slowly, "I am a campesino." He explained how he grew up in the countryside, loved the campesinos, and had always wanted to be of service. Radalme explained how as a boy, he had a big, swollen belly. An American medical team came to his campo and gave him medication to get rid of the parasites in his system.

When the interview was done the committee discussed him. I thought he was perfect. Finally, someone who understood the mission! The Dominicans were concerned about his English skills. Terri said she was the one who would be speaking to him the most in English. "His English is just fine," she said, firmly.

Radalme was hired one day before we returned to Omaha, after we had spent eight months in Santiago. I told Radalme the single most important thing was to listen to Jose Miguel, the man whose salary Mateo had tried to cut. Radalme is still there and so is Jose Miguel. Radalme was an excellent choice. His organizational skills and business and agricultural knowledge have been great assets to the ILAC Mission. Jose Miguel is still the heart of ILAC.

Though the work I have participated in through ILAC has challenged my stamina and my faith, Terri and I are proud to have had a hand in sustaining such an important mission.

Terri also deeply believes in the work we do there. For a number of years, she helped supervise the nursing students. Between 2002 and 2007, she served as the director of the Creighton Institute for Latin American Concern. That last assignment came as a surprise and an honor.

Terri first heard about the new assignment while we were in Spain, visiting her daughter Brenda and her family in 2001. The phone in Brenda's home rang. It was for Terri, which was strange since we were halfway across the world. Not many people we knew had that number. It was one of our Jesuit friends, asking for Terri. The friend asked her to fill in for a few months because the director of ILAC had resigned. When Terri got off the phone that day, I asked, "Who was that?"

"Father Alexander. He wants me to run ILAC for a few months until they find a new director."

"Did you talk about how much you get paid?"

"No," she replied.

"Or what your hours or actual duties will be...or how much time will be spent in the Dominican Republic and how much in Omaha?"

"No."

"Well, what *did* you talk about?"

"We didn't really talk about anything, we just prayed and cried."

Uh oh, I thought. It was a stressful time to be a part of the ILAC program. It was experiencing some major bumps in the road. We didn't quit, though. Just the opposite, actually. The challenges seemed to strengthen our faith in God and in this work. Terri's goal at the time was just to sustain the program, to hold it together for the future, and that's what she did.

Never could we have imagined that we would be in those two positions at the same time, me as interim executive director in Santiago and Terri as the Creighton ILAC Director. It was not in our wildest dreams. Maybe there was a higher calling that we blindly answered. 2002 was a unique time in our lives.

To properly get a handle on the shifting tides of the ILAC program, we were going to need to be there for quite a while. But what would we do with David? It seemed unkind to him and frankly unsafe to leave him behind for several months. There really wasn't any place he could be for that long a time. We also worried about David's health. Malaria was a legitimate concern in that part of the world. It can be harder to know when and how David is sick because he can't tell us what's happening. We worried for weeks about what to do. Then, one night after work, Terri came home and said, "We're just going to take him. People will help us." Terri is prone to epiphanies like this. Usually, she's right.

Here, again, is a portion of Terri's magazine article.

What About David?

It was one thing for Joe, my husband, and me to run off to a Third World country, using two weeks' vacation to live without running water or electricity, but quite another to go for a longer period. We had our Down's child to consider. David, now 30, functions at the level of a three-year-old except that he doesn't talk, feed himself, or do any self-care. We'd once thought he had autism because he is generally withdrawn and especially reserved with strangers and in strange places. He is sweet and loving and happiest when there are no changes in his daily routine: getting up at the same time, eating the same thing, waiting for the bus to go to the workshop, home for dinner with Mom and Dad, then TV and a bedtime routine.

Boy, were we going to change David's routine. Instead of working at ILAC for two weeks, Joe and I were trying to figure out how to go for eight months to work with the students, travel the country, and visit new programs.

"What about David?" was a question we both pondered for three years.

Then one day, a peace came over me. I announced to my husband with certainty, "We'll just take him!"

Our time in the Dominican Republic proved to be an awakening for David, much the same way ILAC has been changing the hearts of students for so many years. He began to smile more, be more independent, and he began to dance! In the Dominican Republic, dance is an integral part of the culture, and David loved the music. David's dance was definitely unique – he'd wiggle and shake and grin from ear to ear – but it did resemble the *merengue.*

"David no habla nada," he doesn't talk at all, I'd tell the Dominicans, but that didn't bother them, they would talk nonstop Spanish to him with their arms around him. One day, Maria, a neighborhood woman, explained it: "*David entiende mucho, el habla de corazon,*" David understands a lot; he speaks from his heart. I choked back tears and said, "*Estoy de acuerdo,*" I agree. He'd hug his Dominican friends and communicate love with special rhythmic pat-pat-pats on their shoulders, pats usually reserved for mom and dad.

David's adjustment was our biggest fear; it turned out to be our greatest joy. He was transformed in a most amazing way that brought to my memory words of Ignatius: "Love consists in sharing what one has and what one is with those one loves. Love ought to show itself in deeds more than words."

For the first eight months in our new positions, Terri, David and I all lived in a small casita at the ILAC Center in Santiago. The rolling hills there contain a kind of peace that cannot be had in the States. David hung out with us in the office. When he wasn't rocking in a rocking chair or visiting with a new friend, he watched movies on the portable DVD player we brought for him. It was a beautiful time for our family.

In 2005, Terri was one of two people to receive the St. Ignatius Award from the president of the university. The award recognized university faculty and staff who exemplify the ideals of St. Ignatius Loyola in their lives and work. Specifically, Terri emphasized the personal and spiritual growth that one receives from serving the people of the Dominican Republic. It was personally awarded on the altar at mass at St John's Church (Creighton's church) by Creighton University President, Father John Schlegel. David and I were there to see her receive the honor. I was so proud of Terri.

VII – More Stories

By now, you get the drift of my work in the Dominican Republic. This work has been a huge part of my life for so many years. As such, there are many stories, some about faith, some about challenges and successes, and some are just funny or strange. Here are a few more.

Statistically speaking, our family should have experienced multiple illnesses for all our time in the developing world. I really don't like to use the word blessed because it is used so often and so casually. However, we have always felt protected when we are in the Dominican Republic. None of us have ever experienced any type of mosquito-borne diseases, though they are common there. There are a lot of mosquitos. Most of our work is for several weeks in the summer when there are even more mosquitos! The Dominican Republic has dengue fever, chikungunya, Zika, and some malaria. We have never sought out medical care for ourselves in the 30+ years of working there, though we have taken a number of students to clinics and hospitals over the years.

In the early years everyone, even we, experienced diarrhea. We experienced only mild cases, but oh boy, did our students and professionals suffer. One summer, we set up a small infirmary on the mission grounds so we could keep some of them back at the mission and attend to them. The theory years ago was to let the diarrhea run its course for a few days, to get rid of whatever triggered the diarrhea. If there was blood in the stool or a fever, we would start medication immediately. The diarrhea can be caused from contaminated food or parasites. It was a guessing game to decide which medication to begin, so usually we would start one. If that did not slow down the diarrhea, then we would start the other one. Of course, staying hydrated and using anti-diarrhea meds were essential. Untreated diarrhea can be fatal. When the mission was built, the kitchen staff was educated about how to use good water to wash vegetables, etc. That made a big difference. Also many of the fruits and vegetables are now grown on the mission property, eliminating potential contamination from outside sources. When we were able to have better sanitation and we wrote up-to-date diarrhea protocol, uncontrolled, untreated diarrhea became rare.

We do have one exceptional story about David and diarrhea. Though some might assume David is at a higher risk for complications from illness in the DR due to his lack of language, he never got sick because we controlled everything that went into his mouth. He doesn't eat or drink from the street vendors. He doesn't risk parasites by eating mangos and other fruit right off the tree. He really only consumed what we gave him and we were very cautious. He never got diarrhea until one day, one time, one spectacular explosion of diarrhea. It happened one evening when we were entertaining professionals by taking several American VIPs to dinner in a nice open-air restaurant in Santiago. David seemed fine until…

After dessert of "dulce de leche," we thought we had better take David to the bathroom before we left. It was a long ride home and he seemed uncomfortable. When in public, I would take David to the boy's bathroom. On the way to the bathroom the floodgates of poop opened up. I could smell what I thought was gas, but no. It was poop streaming down his leg, leaving a trail leading into the bathroom. In the bathroom, he made it to the toilet but the mess was unbelievable. It just was everywhere, in his clothes, on his clothes, socks, shoes, everywhere. It was truly spectacular. There was not much time, nor enough toilet paper or paper towels. Terri yelled in to ask if everything was okay. I tried to explain the disaster at hand. She was able to get more paper towels for the mess but there was no getting everything. We had no change of clothes with us. He just had to wear the soiled clothing. Eventually, I emerged from the bathroom with David. I am sure he felt better than before, but the smell was staggering. Our Dominican driver was waiting with his shiny white van. We tried to explain what happened. Everyone rolled down their windows and held their breath. The group was very kind and understanding. Now we laugh about it. If only David could talk! We have never gone back to that restaurant.

While I'm on the topic of digestive health, I have one more story. One might think the gastrointestinal problems our volunteers experience are limited to the typical traveler's diarrhea. However, constipation can also be a problem. One summer a poor nursing student experienced one of the worst cases of constipation I have ever seen. In the campos, the students stay with the Dominicans in their modest homes. They tend to give our students the very best room. It is not unusual that the family locks everyone in the house during the night. It can be dangerous for anyone, including Dominicans, to go outside to use the latrine at night. This particular student had an aversion to the latrines, and felt embarrassed to use them when so many people were around. At night, she would feel the urge to use the facilities, but she was locked in the house. This went on for many days.

The groups spend two separate two-week blocks of time living in the campos. There is a break of two days between the sessions, and at the end there is a glorious closing ceremony at the mission. She arrived at the ILAC Mission at the end of the second two weeks, reporting to us her gastrointestinal distress. She was bloated, nauseated, and very uncomfortable. We began the normal treatment for constipation, medication, but nothing happened. Then, we went to a *farmacia* or pharmacy to purchase enemas. Again, nothing happened.

By now we were getting ready for the final mass and beautiful closing ceremony, which we love and everyone attends. The church was filled. The Dominicans come with something like pineapple or mangos from their campos to place on the altar. Dominicans and Americans alike are dressed up for this ceremony. Terri and I were trying to figure out what to do next for the student. She was in great pain. The Dean of the Nursing School from Creighton was there visiting. We asked for her advice. She said let's move her to my casita, where there is air conditioning and a private bathroom. How kind, we thought. Yes, we moved her.

Next was an attempt at manual removal of the impaction. Yes, it's as gross as it sounds. Terri and the Dean of the Nursing School did the best they could. Since I am male, I spared her the embarrassment of my involvement. Instead I happily stepped out of the casita and attended the mass. Terri arrived late. The Dean stayed back with the patient. A few minutes after Terri got settled in her seat next to me in the church, the Dean came in and whispered something to Terri. There was a situation. By now, you see, everything had moved but another problem developed. The toilet in her casita was plugged and overflowing. We had a "code brown." The Dean, thinking quickly, turned off the water to the toilet. However, our patient still needed to sit on the toilet. Without going into any further detail, all ended well. Eventually the problem resolved. We were able to participate in the rest of the closing ceremonies with a sigh of relief.

While we laugh about these problems now, it's important to note that without medical treatment, both diarrhea and constipation can be deadly. In the States, we take clean water and sewers for granted. But look what happens to Americans when those utilities disappear. We are not immune, just lucky. One of the services ILAC is devoted to is access to clean water, to avoid parasite contamination. Further, we provide education about sanitation to all the campos to help residents prevent these problems. Hopefully these efforts help prevent long-term problems from untreated gastrointestinal disease.

The one time I did need medical treatment, I was too far away to reach it. It started when Terri and I hiked into Loma Prieta, a stunningly beautiful mountain campo. The hike in was longer and more difficult than I expected. As we approached the campo, villagers and students met us and tried to get me to ride a horse the rest of the way up the mountain. I told them that after coming this far, and working this hard, I was not about to RIDE into the campo on a horse. We had been hiking over three hours. I would walk into the campo. I wanted full credit for making the hike.

That night we had a wonderful bonfire with the Dominican campesinos and students gathered around the fire. Off to my right side, I noted "flashes" of lightning but Terri did not notice it. I changed sides of the bonfire and now the lightning appeared to be from the other direction, still on my right side. After a while, I noted many dark floaters swimming through my right vision field. Finally I realized that there was not really any lightning. It was all coming from my right eye. In the morning the floaters were still there. I got out my Merck manual and read about "detached retina" symptoms and treatment. The symptoms were consistent with mine. It was described as a "medical emergency," requiring immediate care to prevent possible permanent loss of vision, meaning surgery might be required urgently.

I thought it about it awhile and decided that I could not really go anywhere very rapidly, so my decision was really easy, I would just have to see how things went. Terri understood, but kept saying to lie down to keep it from getting worse. In those days, there were no cell phones or roads up to these villages.

The visual symptoms gradually improved. When I got back to Omaha, I saw an ophthalmologist who told me that I had a "healed" detached retina in the right eye. He said, "If I saw you earlier, at the time of initial symptoms, I would have done surgery. It appears to have healed itself so we might as well see how it goes, but call me immediately if those symptoms reappear." It is hard to grasp miracles when they happen to you.

Along the northern border with Haiti, there is a Dominican town called Dajabon. Near there, in the 1930s, along the Massacre River, many thousands of Haitians were killed by the Dominican dictator, Rafael Trujillo, in his attempt to cleanse the Dominican Republic of Haitians. Today communities live on each side of this river. There is occasional tension but it is generally peaceful. Twice a week, approximately 2,000 Haitians are allowed to cross the river into Dajabon to set up tents and makeshift stands to sell their wares to people who come from all over the Dominican Republic. The Haitians and

Dominicans mix, forming a large, noisy, pulsating crowd of sellers, buyers, and onlookers like us. There are many business people from Santo Domingo who hope to buy and resell goods. There are piles of shoes, clothing, and underwear, all new and untouched. There are French perfumes, toiletries, and all types of shirts and athletic shoes, all donations from France and other countries intended for the Haitians. These donations arrive in large shipping containers, but are not handed out to citizens. Instead, Haitians attempt to turn them into cash at the market. They also attempt to sell their own crafts and eggs and other homegrown products.

The day we were there, Terri, David, and I watched this remarkable group of thousands as they milled about, buying, selling, negotiating, laughing, and chattering in different languages. As we walked about, definitely the whitest people there, vendors approached us, pushing forward their wares, hoping we would purchase something, anything. Suddenly, a large very black woman stepped directly in front of Terri, smiled and patted David on the arm. Then another woman appeared and others, patting and talking in Creole and some very accented Spanish that we did not understand easily. With some help from our Dominican driver, Alfie, we learned that all these women had children with Down syndrome or another handicap. They wanted to greet us, welcome us and say hello. They asked with curiosity, "Does he talk? Does he go to school? Does he feed himself? Does he understand what you tell him? How old is he?" They were very attentive and interested in our answers.

The vendors moved away from our special interaction, mothers sharing very personal stories. There were smiles, tears, and gentle hugs, and many pats for David. Eventually, the women moved on. Three o'clock came and Dominican soldiers came. They began pushing the Haitians back across the bridge, sometimes threatening them with large sticks if they moved too slowly. The market was over for the day, but we felt something very special had happened. For just a moment, two very different peoples and cultures had touched, recognized their common humanity and demonstrated affection to each other.

I wish the story ended there, but there is a little more to that day's story. As we were leaving the market area, a very thin woman tried to stop our pickup truck. I think she was begging for food or money. She was a mom, with a baby on her hip. Alfie, our driver, kept going. We didn't make him stop. It upset Terri to pass her by without stopping.

As planned, we continued our journey to the north coast for a weekend on the beach at a nice boutique hotel. Terri could not stop thinking about the haunting images of the day, especially the woman at the end. She was crushed that we did not take time to be present, to listen, and to even try to understand what it must be like to live with such hunger and poverty. The woman was so desperate she tried to stop a moving truck with Americans in it. The contrast of the poor and desperate and the fancy resort were just too much to experience all in the same day. This was true for both of us. Terri cried most of the evening.

As we sat in relative splendor that evening, Terri and I felt all the emotions of our situation wash over us. Guilt. Sorrow. Joy. Exhaustion. We were the lucky ones. We try to help in every way that we can, but sometimes the problems in the DR seem too big. It's not fair that we get to drift in and out, not fair that we were the ones born in the United States and given an education. But what can we do? Like Mari holding the sick child at the clinic that summer, all we can do is offer what we have. That has to be enough because it's all we have to offer.

Chapter 11

Haiti

I – Visiting the Hospitals

Haiti and the Dominican Republic have an unusual relationship. They share the same Caribbean island, Hispaniola. I have visited Haiti a few times and found it exotic, fascinating, and very discouraging.

My first visit was sometime in the mid-1990s when a physician friend and I took a tropical medicine course at Tulane University in New Orleans. We then went to Haiti for a program sponsored by Holy Cross Hospital (Hopital Sainté Croix) in Leogane. Leogane is a few miles from Port-au-Prince, the capital, and about twenty miles from the Haitian/Dominican border.

On the plane to Port-au-Prince I sat next to a gentleman who said he was also going to Holy Cross Hospital. When he said he worked for the Presbyterian Church, I said I thought Holy Cross was Episcopalian. He told me a wonderful story about how in the 1970s, he was part of a group sent by the Presbyterian Church to determine how to identify and implement projects to assist the poor in Haiti. After evaluating the various options, the Presbyterian group recommended supporting the already ongoing projects of the Episcopalian Church in Haiti instead of initiating separate programs. The Presbyterian and the Episcopalian Churches have been working together at Holy Cross Hospital and other areas in Haiti ever since, a beautiful example of interdenominational cooperation to advance common goals.

On a Sunday morning in Leogane, we went to an Episcopalian church. Mass was performed in a rather formal combination of French and Creole, which reminded me of the Latin and English Catholic masses of my childhood. Afterwards, the priest invited us into the sacristy. He was very welcoming and kind. Later, as we walked down a dirt street toward our residence, I was startled by the sudden onset of a loud rhythmic thunder coming from a side street a couple of blocks away. I asked, "What is that?" Our guide said, "Oh, that's the Catholics, they just love the Haitian drums." We walked on without further comment, but I was pleased. I liked the drums, too.

One evening, we went to a large, magnificent Episcopalian Church in Port-au-Prince, for a young people's concert. It was beautiful, with classical music played superbly by young men and women with crisp white shirts and contrasting black skin. I was surprised and very impressed. I wondered how they learned such excellent musicianship while living in Haiti.

Later, a visit to Mother Teresa's hospital for the dying had been arranged for two other physicians and me. They usually did not allow visits, but Holy Cross Hospital had a good relationship with the nuns so they agreed to our visit. We passed through a gate at the bottom of a hill leading to the entrance of the hospital. As we approached the top of the hill, we looked across the valley at the slums. It sounded as if one single Creole voice was echoing across the valley. We learned that the people's radios were all tuned to the broadcast of an ongoing Haitian national team soccer game. We knocked on the entrance door and after a time it was answered by a dark-skinned nun. I recognized her white sari with the three blue strips, the beautiful robe of Mother Teresa's nuns, the Missionaries of Charity. It took my breath away. I thought, *This is the real thing.* We told her who we were and she said, "Please wait."

We sat in the sun, looked over the valley and listened to the Creole broadcast of the soccer game. After an hour or two she returned and said, "You may come in." She introduced us to a couple of other nuns and began leading us through open wards with many beds, all occupied. One area was for dying AIDS patients. Since they were dying, as so many did in those days, I was uncertain how much medical care was appropriate and how much they were doing. I asked, "Do you give the AIDS patients IVs?"

She looked at me, paused, and after a few long seconds, she said, "Yes, doctor, we do the best we can."

I felt terrible and ashamed. I think she thought I was challenging the quality of her treatment. Her, of all people.

Later, she said, "I have a favor to ask. Maybe you could help us." She said that the patients there were expected to die soon. Some came from hospitals, but most were just dropped off at the bottom of the hill and then brought up to their hospital. Most would die before long, but there were some who lived quite some time, even months. They appeared ill, but did not seem to be dying. She asked, "Could you examine them and tell us if any of them have a chance at getting better? We can try to send them to a better hospital." What a request, so very different than how we usually approach patients. We examined chests, palpated abdomens, and listened to hearts and lungs. We found a few that might benefit from further evaluation, but we didn't really know. How could we know? The nuns asked; we tried. A very humbling experience.

During that trip, we also visited a downtown children's school and clinic, a tuberculosis (TB) hospital in Port-au-Prince, and Cardinal Leger Leprosy Hospital near Leogane, run by nuns from Quebec. All were clean and beautifully kept. At the TB Hospital, we were greeted by a large black man in a white lab coat who strode rapidly across the grounds toward us, saying loudly, "You Americans, who brought

AIDS to Haiti, now will not let anyone donate blood if they have been to Haiti in the past two years. Can you believe that? Do you agree with that? How about New York and how about New Jersey, and God only knows about San Francisco."

Startled, I stammered, "I didn't know that. I don't know anything about that, but I don't think I agree." A wide grin crossed his face, he laughed out loud and gave me a hug, saying, "Of course, of course, you don't know anything about that. Come, let me show you around," and off we all went to see the hospital.

II -- Haiti Earthquake, 2010

ILAC is a Dominican program, primarily for Dominicans but there is unavoidable overlap with Haiti and its people. There is a long and complicated history between the two countries, but when the massive earthquake hit Haiti on January 12, 2010, causing massive destruction and killing over 200,000 people, the Dominicans were the first to help. The ILAC Center in Santiago was a staging area for many groups who went on to Haiti. Creighton University Medical Center and Bergan Mercy Hospital sent many groups to the damaged areas for a month following the earthquake.

The Jesuit Refugee Service, based in Dajabon on the Haitian border, was contacted by Father Bill Johnson, a Jesuit based at the ILAC Center in Santiago. He asked, "How can we help?" They suggested going to Jimani, which is on the Dominican side of the Haitian/Dominican border and where a small Baptist medical clinic and facility was located. Jimani is in the DR but only thirty miles from Port-au-Prince and twenty-two miles from Leogane, which was the epicenter of the earthquake. The Dominican border was declared open quickly and Haitians poured across, seeking help. The Creighton/Bergan groups and many others from around the world arrived rapidly.

I asked my friends, "Should I go? Can I help?" They said, "No, no, no. We don't need you, we have lots of doctors. We need nurses and other health professionals who can do hands-on care for the injured." Shortly afterwards, Terri was contacted by one of our friends to go with a group of nurses the next morning, flying directly to Santiago in a private jet, donated by a local business. Terri said, "I have not been doing hands-on nursing, I have been doing administrative nursing the last few years." "Yes, yes, that is exactly what we need. We have a group of nurses going and we need a team leader, someone who can organize and help keep things straight once you get there." Terri, Dr. Theresa Townley, and 14 nurses were quickly on their way, with lots of donated equipment. My niece Janet (DeBacker) Facciano, from Spokane, Washington, also volunteered and worked with the same group. I know having Janet there, a great nurse and family member, was a comfort to Terri.

Terri and Dr. Townley helped organize some of the chaos at the site in Jimani, counseled some of the anxious nurses and helped care for the injured. When Terri arrived, there were 450 patients on the grounds and the conditions were difficult. I did try to assist on a committee helping with communications, supplies, recruiting more professionals, and figuring out how and when to get our volunteers home, since no plans were made how the volunteers were to return when they left so rapidly. Terri did real work while I watched from a distance, which is not all that unusual in our marriage.

Terri and the team returned home after a week. Other teams worked in Jimani for a few more weeks, after which the most seriously injured survivors were transferred by United States Army helicopters to the USNS Comfort, a 1,000-bed hospital ship in Port-au-Prince bay. There is much more to this story but that is for another time.

Haiti continues to suffer and its relationship with the Dominican Republic is strained. Haiti's deep poverty and many problems appear overwhelming to me. I have no idea how to really make things better there, ever. But, as they say, we must try. And many people are trying. I wish them well. They need our prayers.

It is not easy to always appropriately focus on our work. Sometimes, Terri and I recall a quote that has been commonly used for reflections at ILAC:

Holy Ground

"Our first task in approaching another people, another culture, another religion, is to take off our shoes – for the ground we are approaching is holy. Else we may find ourselves treading on men's dreams. More serious still, we may forget that God was here before our arrival."

The original quote, attributed to Max Warren, continues, *"We have to sit where they sit to enter sympathetically into the pains and griefs and joys of their history and see how those pains and griefs and joys have determined the premises of their argument. We have, in a word, to be 'present' with them."*

Max Warren was born in Dun Laoghaire, Ireland, of Irish missionary parents. He spent some of his childhood in India, attended Cambridge, and became a prominent British missionary leader. He died in 1977. He sounds like a very wise and thoughtful man.

Chapter 12

Our Children

I – No Labels

Some blended families refer to their children as "yours, mine, and ours." Terri and I were against that notion. There are no "my children," "her children," or "stepchildren" in our world. We only have our children. We have tried, with intention, to bring our children together as a new family unit. As the years went by, our children married and started their own families.

Mari married Patrick Kucera on May 25, 1990.

Mike married Christine Davids on November 16, 2001.

Ryan married Kristi Lankford on June 11, 1999.

Brenda married Ramon Javier Bescansa Sanjurjo on July 25, 1997.

Between all these beautiful couples, we are lucky to have 16 grandchildren. This new phase of life has presented more opportunities for me to find new ways to love and to be of service. Terri and I want to be anchors in our grandchildren's lives. We want to be present for the good times and the challenging times. We want them to know we are there for all of them—both our adult children and our precious grandchildren. We want all our kids to know they have a soft place to fall. We're the backup team; we're the pinch hitters; we're the cheering section—and we're thrilled about it. We are there for all our kids 100 percent.

Can I tell you how proud we are? We so admire our grown children and their spouses. All are raising their children in the Christian tradition with Christian values. All are engaged as loving parents. All put their children's needs first. All work hard to provide the very best for their kids. I am pleased that all our adult children have stayed married. They chose their spouses carefully, perhaps learning from our problems.

I consider myself very lucky to be close geographically to all the children. Ryan and Mike's families are minutes from our house. Brenda and her husband, Ramon, lived in Spain for five years but have been in the Omaha/Lincoln area since 2004. Mari and Patrick lived in Rockford, Illinois for a few years, but now have been in Kansas City for many years. No matter the distance, we hold them all close.

This proximity facilitates something I didn't really have as a child. Terri and I get to host or attend birthday celebrations, milestones, and holidays, which allows our grandchildren the opportunity to know their grandparents. I didn't realize how important that would be until Terri and I were shopping for houses. Trying to locate a little closer to the kids' families was important. Initially, I thought we would be looking for something smaller, a condo perhaps. Instead, as time went on, I realized that I really wanted a larger home. I finally asked Terri one day, "Do you think we should be downsizing or upsizing?"

She said, "Downsize? The next ten years are the grandchildren years, we're not downsizing!"

"Well, what's your ideal house?" I asked.

"I want all the kids and grandkids to be able to eat within eyesight of each other," she said. I agreed. She wanted holiday meals to include our whole family. She wanted our home to be a place where everyone is included, where there is community. She was right. These days, there can be as many as 30 people at family gatherings. So, there's some overflow, but we can still all see each other. I consider that a blessing.

Our families live in different communities, attend different schools, and have different lives, but we do all share time together, which I enjoy very much. We try to share holidays and birthdays and vacations and special celebrations when we can, whether it is in Omaha, Mexico, The Black Hills, the Great Wolf Lodge in Kansas City, racing in soapbox derbies, or just decorating sugar cookies at Christmas. I was thrilled when another generation of soapbox derby racers emerged. Owen, Ben, Teagan, Liam, Cian, and Shaun, along with other cousins and friends, are all now racing on the track at Seymour Smith Park in Omaha and all are doing very well. I am sure Brielle will be joining them soon.

II – Mari & Patrick Kucera Family

Mari and Patrick have six children, with Mari serving as a stay-at-home mom. She is a hands-on and loving presence. They have faced challenges with style and grace and with an unshakeable faith in God. I guess if I would sum up Mari with one word, it would be Mom. She has an unstoppable, positive spirit. Her favorite phrase is, "It's all good."

Mari and Patrick met in college at Creighton University. I think it was love at first sight. They are a loving couple. Patrick is a loving husband and amazing father. Both Mari and Patrick coached their kids in various sports. All the children are athletic and outdoorsy, which I admire. Patrick is a hunting and camping enthusiast and he has passed these skills on to his children, especially the boys. Every year he leads a large group to Canada for backwoods hunting and fishing.

Their firstborn, Patrick, died in the eighth month of pregnancy, shortly before his expected arrival. He had red hair highlights and was beautiful. He was Mari and Patrick's first child and my first grandchild. Words cannot describe the pain and sorrow of his loss and burial. We miss him and think about what age he would be now.

Joey, or Joseph, is my namesake and also his paternal grandfather's, whose name is also Joseph. He was a beautiful, high-energy baby. He was a welcome new beginning to their family. He excelled in sports, especially soccer. Joey graduated from Kansas State University. He is a great role model for his siblings. He has a sense of adventure, traveling to Australia, New Zealand, Jamaica and Trinidad, and has been an important part of leading the frequent Canada trips with his father. He also loves to write.

Christine, the sweet, responsible second born, was a light from the time she arrived. As a toddler, she was always kind and gentle, always in tow behind Joey. Growing up, Christine always wanted to be Mom's helper, washing dishes or whatever needed to be done. She was a superb soccer player. She graduated from College of the Ozarks. It made me smile to hear she had decided to become a teacher, following in the footsteps of her great-grandparents, my mother and father. She is such a hard worker, balancing service, work, and studies. Christine is a traveler and has spent time volunteering in Africa, Belize, Guatemala, and California, following in my love of service. She has embraced her faith and encounters people with a bright shining light. Christine connects with David in a special way. One time, Terri, David and I went to visit her at college in Branson, Missouri. We all decided to go shopping. David grabbed onto Christine and would not let her go. They have been fast friends ever since. It is not easy to form that kind of a bond with David. He saw that light!

MaryEileen is the youngest of Mari and Patrick's first three children. Joey and Christine always watched out for MaryEileen. She is happy-go-lucky, light-hearted, and a free spirit. She played up on the same soccer teams as Christine throughout school. It was fun to watch the sisters on the field, playing with such intensity. MaryEileen also has fun with David when she visits. She sits on the floor facing him in his rocking chair. David has discovered he can make her laugh and laugh by making "monster faces" at her. It makes me smile to see the two of them rocking in sync and laughing together. She is pursuing her degree at Kansas State. She is an amazing dancer, fun, and studies hard.

Michaela was born in Rockford, Illinois, full term, but stillborn. She was perfect with a beautiful head of hair with a large bow put on by the nurses. I was present with them in Rockford while Mari spent those last precious minutes holding her. It seems to me, looking back, that very few words were spoken. Losing her was such a blow. Another baby buried. Another moment to witness a family showing courage and grace and faith, all wrapped in one tragic package, holding them together. I remember that it was Patrick's birthday on the day of the funeral. It was surreal, singing "Happy Birthday" to Patrick at the luncheon following Michaela's burial…on one of the saddest days imaginable.

Mari's next pregnancy was risky. We were fearful for her. Pregnant with twins, Mari went into labor at 24 weeks (instead of the usual 40 weeks). She was hospitalized to try to keep the labor at bay. The boys were born at 28 weeks, weighing barely two pounds each. Another of life's challenges. Again, we were all on our knees with a prayer that these boys would survive and thrive. They were stabilized in the NICU and came home from the hospital after two months, on oxygen and multiple monitors with lots of help from their church and friends. We came as often as we could. Mari and Patrick handled it with grace and grit.

James came first, followed by his brother, Jeremy. Both were fighters. Both required much care and attention. I waited and watched as they grew up and grew strong. I still consider it a great blessing.

Sometimes I have had trouble telling them apart but I shouldn't, and I do know and love them as individuals.

James can run like the wind. We have heard the expression on the sidelines at his soccer games, "Be careful, James, you'll get a speeding ticket!" He is kind and gentle. He works hard, and loves soccer, baseball, basketball, and the outdoors. In first grade, his teacher mentioned how good it was that he could make people laugh, and he still has that gift. James is finishing high school now, with a promising future.

Jeremy is quieter in a group, but he has a lot to say when anyone mentions football. He excels at football, and boy can he run! They both seem to have inherited that running gene. Jeremy didn't have much blocking in his last football season, but still made Sunflower League honorable mention running back. He is also a very good wrestler. Both sports have given him some tough injuries, but he just gets up again, keeps going, and does well. Jeremy's football teammates respect him and like him. They even voted him team captain. He is a leader and a constant worker and will do well.

Josh is the family's millennium baby, born in February 2000. The twins were still being closely monitored. All went well with his delivery and he was such a mellow baby, a perfect fit for this bustling family. He too, like all the Kucera kids, is blessed with athletic ability. He has played on soccer teams with the twins for many years. What a thrill to see them all on the field at the same time, working together seamlessly, making a difference as only three siblings could. Josh, too, loves the outdoors and the Canada trips. Josh is in high school. He has a gift for computers, robotics and academics. He too, can be quiet, especially when all his siblings are around.

After realizing that I was missing chances to talk to all the kids in the big crowd, I decided I would like to take each of the kids alone, just for a few minutes when we all get together. I love to hear what they have to say that maybe can't be said when there are six kids gathered together. It's important to me that they all have a relationship with their grandfather. I want to know them as individuals and to hear what they're thinking about. The time spent talking has been a gift to me. I hope it has made a difference for them too.

All the Kucera boys have Patrick as their middle name after their dad and, maybe, in my humble opinion, to honor their first brother.

III – Mike & Christine Lynch Family

Mike, a talented software engineer, met his wife Christine at work. They were both working at a computer corporation. Mike says he was ready to get married when he met Christine—another God-incident, I think. Christine is a great match for Mike. She laughs at his jokes and fun-loving spirit. They started their family in Omaha. Christine had graduated from Truman State University and has her master's degree from the University of Missouri. Mike graduated from the University of Nebraska in Lincoln and is presently taking postgraduate courses.

Benjamin Cole (Ben), their firstborn, came when his cousins were also coming into the world. He was eager to learn and play with all of them. Ben loves to read. He never goes anywhere without a book. Sports and books are his love. Ben played baseball on a select team, and also played basketball and soccer. He is in junior high school. Ben is a good student and enjoys music and playing the viola. Ben is a little on the quiet side, but I have learned to ask him about the book he is currently reading. Then he has a lot to say!

Teagan Courtney was a dream baby, sleeping easily and always happy. She had some trouble with reflux as a baby but still didn't fuss much. Now she is 11 years old—the only girl—and she loves pink and purple. Her room is covered with stuffed animals and frilly décor in her favorite colors. We were with them in Chicago when

Teagan got her very first American Girl doll. For several years, Terri, Teagan, and Christine would go to the annual American Girl fashion show in Omaha. Every trip guaranteed a new outfit or accessory when they arrived home. Teagan has a love of soccer and has excelled in the sport. It is always a pleasure to watch her play. She also enjoys soapbox derby racing and has a great chance to go to nationals in Akron. She has already won four first-place trophies this year. She makes a great sister, especially to Shaun, her younger brother. She is like a second mom to him with a loving, gentle touch. Teagan is also a good student and loves to read. Teagan is learning to play both the cello and trombone. She is in fifth grade.

Shaun Christian, from day one, was full of energy and sweetness. When he could barely talk, he would say "I love you," and give you a big hug. He could outrun us, even as a toddler. You know when Shaun is in the room as he declares himself ready for fun. He was using an iPad before I knew what an iPad was! Shaun is 8 years old, and loves to play with his friends. We pick up the three of them once a week when they have an early out from school.

IV – Ryan & Kristi Lynch Family

During college, Ryan met Kristi while both were doing an internship summer program at the *World Herald* newspaper company in Omaha. Ryan was at Creighton University and she was attending the University of Nebraska in Lincoln. I think they were smitten with each other immediately. I think it's interesting that the two of them were born within two days of each other (Sept. 3, 1975 for Kristi and Sept. 5, 1975 Ryan). They were both born at the same hospital, the old St Joseph Hospital on 10th and Martha Street, where I was practicing medicine. In those days, mothers stayed in the hospital for three or more days, so we are pretty sure they were in the nursery together. Maybe that attraction began very early! Ryan graduated from Creighton University, got married, and started his first job all in the same month. He also has his master's degree from Bellevue University (Nebraska). He is a successful Operations Manager for a small software company. Kristi graduated from the University of Nebraska in Lincoln and also has an MBA from University of Nebraska in Omaha.

Their first child is Owen Ryan, a mini Ryan in looks and mellow temperament. Owen is the oldest of four. I remember him being a happy baby, quiet but observing everything around him. As the years passed and more babies came, Owen assumed the high position of role model and loving big brother. He is a good student in junior high school. He loves baseball and football, school, and enjoys the trumpet. Owen has done very well in soapbox derby racing, with many victories. He has finished second twice in the Nebraska championships, in junior division and also in senior division, literally by two and one inches, respectively. Always a best friend to everyone near him, he is a pleasure to be around. He serves as an altar boy and attends St Patrick's School. Owen is thoughtful and mature beyond his years.

Liam Robert, second born, has a gentle heart. He is aware of feelings and is compassionate. When he took first communion, it was special for him. He delighted in going to the Christian gift shop and pointing out holy things he wanted for his first communion celebration. Terri describes a time when she was taking him somewhere in the car, just age 3, when the rosary was being said on the radio. She quickly changed the station to something more upbeat. Liam exclaimed, "No, turn it back!" Now he is an altar server at St. Patrick's school masses and Sunday masses. Being a middle child for a number of years, Liam is the "keeper of all things fair." That works out most of the time for all his siblings. He enjoys basketball, soccer, football, acting and chess. He is a very competitive chess player and often ranks very high in the tournaments. He also plays saxophone. He has continued his family tradition of excellence in soapbox derby racing.

Cian Joseph, the third boy, is fun, feisty, and well...you know where he stands. When Cian was about 4 or 5 years old, Terri brought him with her to my clinic. He declared to the staff that he would be the next Dr. Lynch. After all, his middle name is Joseph. Dr. C.J. Lynch, please. He is 9 years old, a firecracker, sweet and assertive! When his baby sister was born, he immediately added caring and loving to his repertoire. No signs of jealousy, he just loved that baby girl. He enjoys sports such as football, baseball, and soccer.

After Cian, the family experienced a miscarriage. It was hard to express ourselves to our daughter-in-law and son, how sad we were for them. Terri and I didn't know what to say or do.

Then Brielle Cecilia (Cecilia was my mother's name) was born. Brie's birth gave the family joy. Not only did the family have a healthy, happy baby, but it was a girl! Brie is four now and she is in charge of her brothers. She has them wrapped around her little finger, and they happily oblige. From the time before Brie could talk, she had a special relationship with David. She played a game of running around his rocking chair and giggling. Then she would just plop on his lap for hugs. She is so kind and loving to David, and David loves her too. Brie is a girly girl who loves to dress up, paint her fingernails, and wear lots of fancy shoes. With her blonde hair and energetic personality, she is a mini Kristi.

V – Brenda & Ramon Bescansa Family

Brenda was starting her junior year at Creighton University when her mother and I began dating. She was accepted in the first Creighton University Dominican Republic Semester program, and spent a semester and the following summer at the ILAC Mission in Santiago.

She picked up Spanish quickly. When she returned to Omaha she met her future husband, Ramon Bescansa, a Spaniard, who was in Omaha studying at UNO (University of Nebraska in Omaha). She graduated from Creighton University and went on to graduate from law school at the University of Nebraska. Ramon graduated from University of Nebraska at Omaha (UNO) and is presently working on his master's degree.

During those years while Brenda was engaged to Ramon and finishing law school in Lincoln, Mike was also working on his degree at University of Nebraska in Lincoln. The two of them came up with the idea of sharing an apartment. Brenda had a small extra bedroom in her apartment and Mike had just lost his roommates. We thought the arrangement would save us some money on rent, so we liked the idea. I think Brenda liked the idea of a big brother. We said yes, as long as it didn't negatively affect their relationship. We stressed that their relationship was more important than what we would save on providing separate apartments. The plan seemed to work out. They are still good friends and joke about silly things that happened when they were roommates, such as enthusiastic discussions about thermostat settings. Other stories we will leave untold!

After Brenda finished law school, she and Ramon were married. Then, Flora Elizabeth Bescansa Luers was born two years later in Omaha, a beautiful curly-dark-haired Spanish-looking baby. When she was two months old, Brenda and Ramon moved to Spain to be near his large and loving Spanish family. They lived in Spain for five years. Flora became bilingual at a young age. Flora, now 17 years old, is talented in singing, piano, violin, dance, and color guard. She is also academically gifted, as even a short conversation with her will reveal.

The family's second child is Helen Teresa Bescansa Luers. Helen, Terri's namesake, was born by the sea in northern Spain. They moved back to the States when she was only 2. She loves all things from the ocean, including "pulpo" or octopus, mussels, shrimp, and anchovies. Helen was a quiet, sweet baby. She is now 14 years old. She is compassionate and loves animals. She volunteers at the zoo, and has a pet rat named Taj and a gecko lizard named Nova. She is very artistic and she gives wonderful hugs.

Lucia (Lucy) Aurora Bescansa Luers was born in Omaha. She is the happy-go-lucky, playful youngest child, currently 10 years old. She and Helen have built elaborate cities with play mobile characters and both have a creative play imagination. Lucy loves to read and listen to audio books, draw and write stories about dragons. She wants to become an author. She, too, is artistic and loves her pet chinchilla named Comet. She plays the piano and entertains their two cats, Pepper and Luna.

VI – David Matthew Luers

I have described David, in part, earlier. Because he lives with Terri and me, he is a big part of our daily lives. He is sweet, loving, gives pat-pat-pat-hugs easily, but is non-verbal and needs lots of hands-on care. I get him up in the morning, shave and dress him, feed and get him on the bus to Madonna's sheltered workshop every weekday. In Terri's retirement, she loves sleeping in! She does everything else to care for him, while the morning routine gives David and me some personal time together. David has a "job" at Madonna. He also has friends who are developmentally disabled, who he has play dates and fun events to socialize with, as well. Overall, his health is good, no heart problems, but he has significant gastrointestinal issues that we treat. He is becoming more stubborn as he ages, so that presents challenges. Now, David has a service dog that walks with him (David has some vision problems) and serves as a companion. His dog, Beau, is a rescued greyhound the size of a small deer. Beau has added another dimension to our life. We decided Beau needed a friend, more on the playful side, so we got a rescued female greyhound from the Humane Society. We named her Bella. The two of them love to run, but they mostly want to be near their forever family.

Afterword

In some ways, writing this biography of my life has been very hard. Revisiting old memories reminds me of times I wish I had done better. The project has also reinforced for me how much I miss my mother and my sister—and how I wish I'd had more time with my father. The experience has also been beautiful in ways. Many of my memories are happy. It was fun to think back on my children as audacious young people, their vibrancy and love for life just emerging. Reliving my early relationship with Terri reminded me just how lucky I am to have found her. And there are medical colleagues and mentors I am so happy to be able to honor in this small way.

I started this book project because I realized when reading my family history stories that I wished I knew the reasons behind my parents' and grandparents' big life decisions. I had the what, but not the why. I wanted my family to understand my thoughts, not just my deeds. It was also important to me to put all my family stories in one place. Seeing them strung together like this helps me see how connected I am to those early Lynch pioneers who homesteaded in Nebraska.

I also wanted to honor that 4' 10" blue-haired mom who looked like a grandmother instead of a mom to most people, who in many ways was lost without Dad, but never quit trying to make something special of me. We were a team of two, finding God, maybe not in all things, as the Jesuits like to say, but we found love and warmth in the communities, schools and the churches in all those little towns.

I had a mother who loved me, cared deeply about my future, and wanted me to be a normal boy. I had fun and made life-long friends when we finally settled in Toppenish, Washington. I was fortunate that my mother and people in my life guided me to get a good education. Maybe it was God's grand plan, but maybe I was a lucky boy, as well. Lucky to have opportunities, lucky to have a mother and father who were teachers, who appreciated literature and the arts even when living in towns of a few hundred people in Nebraska or South Dakota, and later, after Dad died, in the Pacific Northwest. Mom taught me many things, including that money was important and anyone who says it is not...well, they have never been without it.

I have been blessed with wonderful children, all our children, and 16 grandchildren. I was lucky to work with the Jesuits and to stumble into the Creighton ILAC program in the Dominican Republic at a time in my life (going through the divorce) when I needed a "life giving, faith-filled purpose." I have been lucky to serve and be served by the Dominicans for over 30 years. Now, I am lucky to be retired, to have good health and the ability to travel. A blessed man to be in my "golden years," surrounded by people I love and who hopefully love me. A lucky boy, humbled by all the goodness around me.

Acknowledgements

I want to thank Corey Radman for her encouragement, perseverance, humor and especially her writing talents. I will always be grateful. Thanks also to Mark Graham for his professionalism and friendship and to Colin Graham for his patience and expertise in organizing and finishing the book. I could not possibly have completed the book without the editorial support, writing skills and consistent encouragement of my wife, Terri. As is true in so many areas of my life, she was a special motivating force.

I leave a lifetime of appreciation and affection to Creighton University where I spent my entire professional career. Creighton really is family to me.

Thanks to all involved with the Institute for Latin American Concern,(ILAC), especially Father Ernesto Travieso, SJ, who got me involved, the ILAC staff at Creighton and in the Dominican Republic and all the volunteers who served over the years. I have a special affection for the Dominicans, a handsome and generous people. I share your love for your beautiful island. Terri and I are so fortunate to know you. A special thank you goes to Father Andy Alexander, SJ, who was very helpful and supportive during difficult times.

I especially appreciate my cousin, Mary Jenks, of Rancho Palos Verdes, California, who generously shared her extensive knowledge of our common ancestry. Thanks to Mary and my cousin, Bob O'Malley, of Murphy, Idaho for forwarding O'Malley information and to my great niece, Tara McAloon, of Spokane, Washington for sharing her letter from her grandmother. Also, thanks and respect to Doris Lynch-Bowers, born 1919, of Arnold, Nebraska and her daughter, Dr. Karolyn (Lynch) Duponcheel, Ed.D. of Ainsworth, Nebraska for their love of family. I appreciate the kindness of Mrs. Jane Kuehn of Heartwell, Nebraska, especially for personally making available the Heartwell Room in the Kearney County Historical Museum. Thanks also to Jack Hultgren at the Jensen Memorial Library in Minden, Nebraska.

I would like to reference "McDowells in America", Gateway Press, Inc., 1981, for ancestry information. I found "The Klu Klux Klan in Nebraska, 1920-1930", by Michael W. Schuyler, Nebraska History 66 (1985): 234-256, to be particularly interesting and informative. There is much information available about the activity of the Klu Klux Klan in Nebraska.

To those many special people in my life who are not included in the book. I have not forgotten you and I am grateful.

Finally, I would like to emphasize my love and gratitude to my wife Terri, who has her own very special story, working her way from Broken Bow and Wahoo to Omaha, where she re-energized my life and became the dynamic component of our charmed and enchanted life together.....The End.

PEDIGREE CHART

Name Joseph Daniel Lynch
Address
City, State
Date

CHART NO.

NO. 1 ON THIS CHART IS THE SAME PERSON AS NO. ____ ON CHART NO. ____

(OVERVIEW) DIRECT LINES

FATHER OF 1

2 Patrick Francis Chester Lynch
B
W
M
W
D
W

4 Philip Wilfred Lynch
B
W
M
W
D
W

8 Patrick Lynch — Cont. on chart #
B 1822–1884
W County Longford, Ireland
M
W
D
W

9 Margaret McDermott — Cont. on chart #
Ireland
B
W B? c. 1896 or 97
D
W

5 Catherine Veronica McDowell
B
W
D
W

10 Bernard (BARNEY) McDowell — Cont. on chart # 1831 B, 1910 d
BORN ?
W Belfast Ireland OR Co. Down Ireland OR Scotland
M
W
D
W

11 Mary Ellen Hughes — Cont. on chart #
B New Orleans 1834 or 35
W
D
W

1 Joseph Daniel Lynch
B
W
M
W
D
W

Mary Ellen Terese (Terri)
NAME OF SPOUSES

MOTHER OF 1

3 Cecilia Agnes O'Malley Lynch
B
W
D
W

6 William O'Malley
B
W
M
W
D
W

12 Austin O'Malley — Cont. on chart #
B 1828–1915
W Co. Sligo Ireland
M
W
D
W

13 Margaret O'Malley — Cont. on chart #
B Co. Roscommon, Ireland
W
D
W

7 Mary Agnes(?) Fitzgerald
B
W
D
W

14 Michael Fitzgerald — Cont. on chart #
Ireland
B
W
M
W
D
W

15 Mary Grace — Cont. on chart #
Ireland
B
W ~~7/~~
D
W ? Co. Kilkenny

LEGEND
B — DATE OF BIRTH
W — WHERE
M — DATE OF MARRIAGE
D — DATE OF DEATH
EVEN NOS. = MALES
UNEVEN NOS. = FEMALES
— EXCEPT NO. 1

Philip W. and Catherine McDowell Lynch, July 1887. Lee Park, Custer County, Nebraska. Grandparents of Joseph Lynch

Philip W. Lynch and Catherine Veronica McDowell Lynch, 1887, wedding picture (my grandparents)

Dec 26th 1898
Lee Park Neb

My Son Chester

Remember well and bare in mind that a true friend is hard to find and when you have found one that is true exchange not the old one for the new.

Philip W. Lynch

Note from my grandfather, Philip W. Lynch, to my father, Patrick Francis Chester Lynch, who was 6 years old.

The Big House, near Oconto, Nebraska

Lynch home place (Philip W. Lynch), near Oconto, NE.

Philip and Catherine Lynch and their five adult children: Patrick Francis Chester Lynch, Sister Marceline (Katherine Lynch), Philip W. Lynch, Catherine McDowell Lynch, James Lynch (back), Ignatius Lynch, Leo Lynch

My father, Patrick F. Chester Lynch, my mother,
Cecilia Agnes O'Malley Lynch, Ignatius Lynch, unknown, Sister Marceline

Sunday afternoon at the Big House. My father is second from right,
my mother is fifth from right in back row, beside Philip W. Lynch

Lynch baseball team, James Lynch seated,
Ignatius with bat, 1920 – 25

St. Mary's Church, Oconto, NE, built in 1912

Stained-glass window by my grandparents, Philip W. and Catherine Lynch, dedicated to his parents, Patrick and Margaret Lynch, my great-grandparents, 1912

Stained-glass window inscription. "In Memory of Patrick and Margaret Lynch," St. Mary's Church, Oconto, NE

Philip W. Lynch and Catherine V. McDowell Lynch

Michael and Mary Grace Fitzgerald, my great-grandparents. Irish immigrants.
Picture approximately 1852

William O'Malley family home, William O'Malley at right. From left are:
Thomas, Anna, Cecilia (my mother), Mary and Jack.

Children of William and Mary Agnes Fitzgerald O'Malley

Wm O'Malley Jr Family

1 Michael 1881 – 1964
2 Peter 1883 – 1918
3 Edward 1884 – 1953
4 Margaret 1886 – 1964
5 Anna 1888 1954
6 William 1890 1916
1970
7 Mary 1892
1914
8 Thomas 1894
9 Cecelia 1896
10 John 1898 1969

Names of O'Malley children

My mother with her sisters and their mother. Back row: Margaret O'Malley Potter, Cecilia O'Malley Lynch, Mary O'Malley; front row: Mother, Mary O'Malley, Anna O'Malley Brennan (My mother is in the center of the back row)

Dad in class play, "The Dear Boy Graduates," 1913, Lexington, NE H.S. Dad is far right in back.

Dad and his sister Katherine
(later Sr. Marceline)

Patrick Francis Chester Lynch (my father)

Dad sitting under his father's picture in The Big House

Mom, Grand Island, NE, High School Graduation, 1916

Mrs. Mary A. O'Malley
announces the marriage of her daughter
Cecilia Agnes
to
Mr. Chester P. Lynch
Wednesday, the thirtieth day of August
nineteen hundred and twenty-two
Grand Island, Nebraska

At Home
after October first
Heartwell, Nebraska

Grandma O'Malley and my mother. My sister, Pat, is the child in front.

Peg and Pat

1932 Heartwell, NE H.S. basketball team. Dad is back left.

1940 Heartwell, NE H.S. baseball team. Dad in back on right.

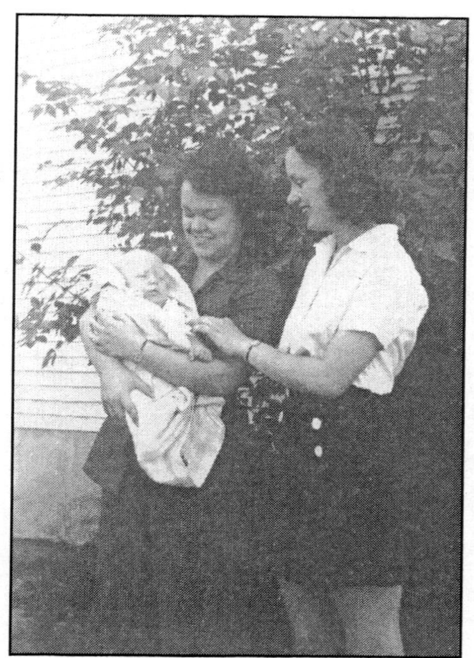

Me, Pat and Peg

My childhood home until age five in Hastings, NE

Dad, Pat, Sr. Marceline, Mom and me, 1944

Pat and Dick DeBacker wedding. I am on right
(I refused to give the priest the wedding ring), 1946.

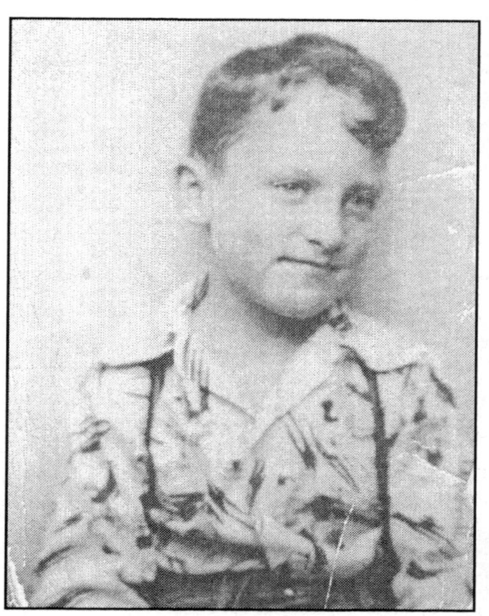

Me age 5

Dad and me in
Okaton, South Dakota, 1948

Me, 1st Communion,
St. Maries, Idaho, 2nd grade, 1949

My aunt, Sr. Marceline, my cousin,
Fr. Leo Sweeney S.J.,
and Grandma Lynch

Bay Center, Washington, 1953, 6th grade. I am far right.

Bay Center, Washington, 1953 school picture, grades 1 – 8. My mother is on far right, behind third row. I am 6th from left in second row. I am in 6th grade.

Marquette High School, Yakima, Washington, Class of 1959,
my high school graduation picture

Mom (Cecilia Agnes O'Malley Lynch), 1965

Me with five oldest DeBacker children, 1954: left to right, back row: Patrice, Susan, me; in front: Mary, Jerry, Janet (being held by me). I was 12 years old.

De Backer Family, my sister, Pat and her husband, Dick and their 11 children: Back row, left to right: Janet, Mary, Dianne, Dick, Pat, Patrice, George Crump (husband of Susan), Susan. Middle row, left to right: Bill, John, Jerry. Front row: Joyce, Laura, Julie

Robert and Margaret (Peg) O'Malley McFadden family
Back row: Terrie, Greg, Cathy, Joan
Front row: Peg, Tim, Bob (Robert)

McFadden children as adults, Thanksgiving 2011,
left to right: Terrie, Greg, Cathy, Joan and Tim (both parents deceased)

Rural Dominican Family, 1982. Fr. Don Doll, S.J.

Arroyo del Toro, Dominican Republic, 1988,
patients waiting outside clinic to be seen

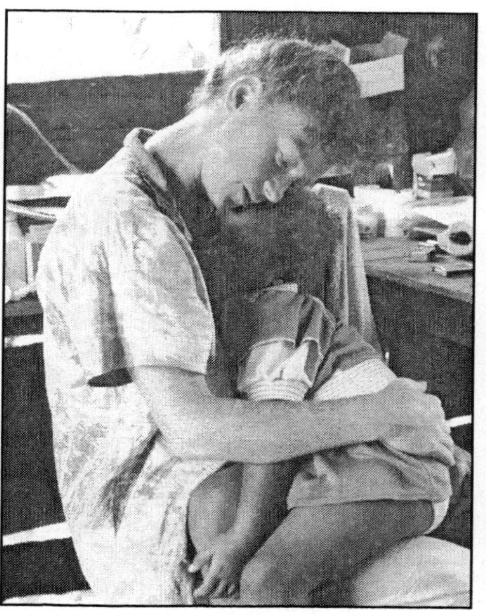
Mari Lynch and Dominican child,
Agua de Juan,
Dominican Republic, 1989

With my daughter, Mari Lynch,
1989, in Dominican Republic

Leogane, Haiti, Tuberculosis Hospital, 1992

4 News THE CREIGHTONIAN 11 February 2005

The Rev. John P. Schlegel, S.J., presents Teresa Lynch, director of the Institute for Latin American Concern, with the St. Ignatious Award at the Alumni Mass on Feb. 6. Lynch is pictured with her husband and son.

The Rev. John Schlegel, S. J., President of Creighton University, presents Terri Lynch, Director of the Institute for Latin America Concern, with the St. Ignatius Award, 2005 at St. John's Church on campus.

Terri Lynch, Haiti Earthquake, January 2010, Jimani, Dominican Republic (border town near Haiti earthquake epicenter)

Terri at orphanage near Morogoro, Tanzania, 2007

Peg, Pat and me, 1996, at Pat and Dick DeBacker's
50th Wedding Anniversary party

Pat and I, 2000

Toppenish High School, class of 1959, 40th Reunion,
Jim Strom, me, George Long

Me at Greeley, NE Irishfest, 2015

Terri, David and I, 2007

Terri and I, 2015

Fr. Scott Hendrickson, S.J. and myself at Oxford University, 2010

Emeritus faculty promotion with Fr. Daniel Hendrickson, S.J.,
President of Creighton University, 2016

Our children and their spouses: Ryan & Kristi Lynch, Christine & Mike Lynch, Joe & Terri Lynch, Ramon Bescansa & Brenda Luers, and Mari and Patrick Kucera, 2013, at my Medical School Alumni Merit Award presentation, Creighton University

David and I with our greyhounds, Bella and Beau

Grandchildren, left to right: Joey, MaryEileen, Christine, Jeremy, James, Josh, Flora, Owen, Ben, Helen, Liam, Teagan, Lucy, Cian, Shaun, 2009 (Brielle was not born yet)

Brielle Cecilia Lynch, our youngest grandchild, Christmas 2016, age 4

Our Family, 2009

Toppenish, Wn.
Jan. 30, 1959

The Benevolent and Protective Order
of Elks.
Yakama, Washington:

Gentlemen:

I will try to give a brief picture of Joseph Lynch's life and background.

He was born in Hastings Nebraska. His father was a professor. He died of a heart ailment at the age of fifty-four. Joseph was then six years old. His two older sisters were married.

There was an outstanding quality about his father. He was always very well liked by the people with whom he worked.

To support myself and Joe I began teaching and came West. Our home life

Moms summary of my life up to 1959
(Recommendation for Elks Scholarship)

has not been ideal and we have lacked many modern conveniences, but he has had the necessities and about all he ever wanted.

He is now facing college. I have little doubt that he will be able to carry the work scholastically. His teachers and I have made every effort to develop in him the knowledge of his obligation as a real Christian and citizen of a democracy.

Sincerely,

Mrs Cecilia Lynch

Moms summary of my life up to 1959 (pg. 2)
(Recommendation for Elks Scholarship)

1

Dear Tara:

My brother & Susan have been on me to write about my Childhood. I was 18 & in College when Joe was born so he doesn't know what I am talking about in Heartwell, ~~Ocinto~~ Oconto, etc - So would you please put on the computer what I write & I will try to get it done -

Was born 2-4-24 at home in Heartwell, NE, the population was about 200. My Dad was the Superintendent of the school and he loved Heartwell, the people and everything about it. My Mother was supposed to teach but she became pregnant with me so the relatives all said her St Joseph Statue she had hung above the bed didn't work (old joke)

When I was 2 years old My cousin Margaret O'Malley (Peg) Came

Patricia Lynch De Backer letter to granddaughter Tara about living in Heartwell, NE in the 1930's

Typewritten copy of my sister Pat's complete letter to her granddaughter, Tara McAloon, 1998
(Original was handwritten)

Page 1

Dear Tara:

My brother & Susan have been on me to write about my childhood. I was 18 & in College when Joe was born so he doesn't know what I am talking about in Heartwell, Oconto, etc. – So would you please put on the computer what I write & I will try to get it done –

Was born 2-4-24 at home in Heartwell, NE, the population was about 200. My Dad was the Superintendent of the school and he loved Heartwell, the people and everything about it. My mother was supposed to teach but she became pregnant with me so the relatives all said her St. Joseph statue she had hung above the bed didn't work (old joke).

When I was 2 years old, my cousin Margaret O'Malley (Peg) came to live with us. She was 10 months old, her Mother had just died and they had 3 kids – Jack & Mary O'Malley were the parents & Jack was my mother's younger brother. They said she was my sister and they raised her through high school. So, I had a playmate and life was fun.

My Dad built a tennis court on the south lot & I remember people came over & they had fun. The place had a cistern with a pump by the back door. Dad figured out how to bring water into a sink in the kitchen. The sink had one faucet and one turned on the water by pushing a button on an electric plate. That turned on a motor in the basement. The motor had a belt that went around a bicycle wheel and that machine pumped water into the sink.

Page 2

No one else had a rig like that & neighbors called it "Chester's invention" but we had water inside the house. Our outhouse was different. It was a long, low shed with three doors – the first door or room was the coal shed, the middle one a toilet with high and low 2 holers, the third door was storage. I still have my Dad's trunk that was in that shed.

In the spring of my fourth grade, Dad was told he was no longer at the school next year. He had coached a winning basketball team and he asked for a raise. They said they couldn't afford him. Mom's version – the Ku Klux Klan was moving around and 2 new men on the school board were in the Klan and the Catholics were let out. So the next three years were tough. The years were 1933, 34, & 1935. Drought years, dust storms, heat and nobody in Heartwell had any money. Dad worked the section gang on the Burlington RR part time, worked on farms, helped on his folks' farm. No money and finally got on W.P.A. A Works Projects Administration job that he got 45.00 a month or 50.00 when he was foreman. He tried getting teaching jobs elsewhere but no luck.

From the first through the seventh grade, I was the only girl in my class, so had to play ball and do whatever the boys did. Saturday we had Catechism at the church. Those classes were large. I was embarrassed about my Dad not having a steady job. The summer before the 8th grade, he got a job on a well drilling outfit on the Burlington RR. However, he was gone all the time.

Page 3

I have a prayer book that he wrote the dates and towns where he was working.

My mother, Jack, Mary & Anna & Margaret (brothers and sisters) sued & Mike O'Malley for their share of the mothers estate. It was settled and each got some money out of it. That paid some bills but Mom was determined to get out of Heartwell where she could get a job and we could go to a Catholic school. Dad was gone and Mom & Peg & I would get in the 1928 Chrysler and we would tour Minden, Kearney, Hastings and Grand Island. She decided on Hastings because she liked St. Cecilia's. One hot day she was parked at the Business College (& why I don't know) and left Peg & me in the car. We got out and some kid squirted us with the hose. The first day at school that kid was in Peg's class – Dick DeBacker.

She bought a house at 812 W 14th in Hastings and we moved. The tennis courts were across the street and the kids were friendly. Peg and I started to school at St. Cecilia's. It was 10 blocks and had to walk home for lunch. She had looked at a house 2 blocks from school but she didn't want to live that close. So we had to walk. Peg & I made friends & we liked Hastings.

Dad came home in October from the well drilling outfit & had been laid off. He liked the house and started doing work on it. His name was never on the title.

Mom could not find a job but she made friends. Peg & I got babysitting jobs. Dad couldn't find work, so started talking about moving up to the Lynch farm.

Page 4

His brother Ignatius (single had died the year before), Grandpa was blind & they knew he could save the farm. They were in dire straits, Dad honestly thought he could do it right and the drought had to end.

Chapter II
Custer Co – Oconto, NE 1937

In Feb or March, Dad loaded his clothes and tools into the Chrysler, and moved up to his parents' farm. The farm was 10 miles south of Oconto, near a Lutheran Church & a deserted place called Buffalo, NE – Lexington, NE is about 20 miles south.

Peg & I were having a good time at school, I was taking sewing from a class at the Y taught by a teacher from the college. My first pattern was slacks, short shorts and a halter. Mom thought I should have made a dress or skirt. I like what I made. Meanwhile my mother made plans for us to move up there. The house had 4 bedrooms, she moved all the furniture into one of the bedrooms upstairs with Peg & my help. My comment was the same as yours, Tara. "My mother is trying to kill us." The day after school was out, we took the train from Hastings to Oconto. Grandpa (Dick DeBacker) & Eddy Laurence came to the depot to tell us goodbye. We only had 2 suitcases & 2 boxes so we didn't bring much.

Dad met us in the Chrysler and explained to us that Grandma had made an apartment for us in the big house Well, when we drove the 10 miles out, we went into a dining room door. She had made the dining room into a combination kitchen/dining room and the stairs to upstairs were in the dining room. We also had the four bedrooms upstairs.

Page 5

Grandma & Grandpa had the kitchen with sink, bathroom, bedroom, and parlor. All the doors shut and locked to the dining room. Their apartment had 3 doors to the outside and basement stairs.

So we were to use the outside toilet, get water from outside & the upstairs was a mess. Anyway Mom was upset, started yelling about "where did she do laundry and dishes, etc." She went upstairs and stayed in the back bedroom for about 2 days. Dad fixed a meal on the coal oil stove. He prided himself on the fact that he never raised his voice. But I rather sympathized with Mom. Anyway, Grandma knocked on the door and invited us in to see Grandpa and gave us doughnuts and tea.

The next day Mom had cooled down and she cleaned and rearranged furniture upstairs. Dad took Peg and me on a tour of the farm. We could even see it was bad. The tractor didn't work and he had planted and cultivated with 4 old horses who were on their last legs. The chickens were a mess, pigs had a disease, and the windmill didn't work right or the pump to the house wasn't working or something. Practically all the peach trees were dead, also the grape vines. Grandpa always had bee hives but they had not been taken care of. We repeated all this to Mom and she said, "Well we will just have to help Dad to get it organized and cleaned up. Peg, you work with me and Pat, you work with your Dad. Dad was delighted about all this. It rained a little that night and that was the last rain all summer.

Page 6

Mom decided that she would cut down a dead peach tree every day and make a wood pile. She couldn't stand the dead trees and by Sept. she had a pretty good sized wood pile. She used a 2 man saw – Peg or me on the other end.

I had only short shorts and a halter to wear and loved getting a great tan. This outfit bothered my Grandmother a lot and she would send me in the house or barn if anyone came and talked to me about modesty and purity. There wasn't a kid within 10 miles all summer.

The dog died and one of the horses. Mom said there was a "meaugh" on the place. Meaugh is Irish for a <u>curse</u>. After the dog was gone, the coyote would raid the chicken house. There were about 38 or 40 cows and one bull. Two of the cows were milk cows, so we had milk, cream, butter, and buttermilk but not enough to sell. Only 6 or 8 eggs a week.

Surprisingly, Peg and I had a lot of fun. We explored the canyons. Grandma had a basket with Indian arrowheads and rattlesnake rattles and we were always looking for Indian heads. We brought in cows. I worked with Dad a lot, he let me drive all over in the Chrysler with the stick shift. He tried to explain why Grandma was like she was. Loss of son, Grandpa blind, and losing the farm.

The thrashers came one day and cut the oats. Peg and I shucked oats and I learned I could work faster than my dad. Every day there was hot sun.

Page 7

We did go to Pressy Park a couple times to swim in the river on the Loup River between Oconto and Broken Bow.

In August the pastures were dried out and Sweeneys came up from Grand Island and bought the cows except the two milk cows and the bulls. Also they bought furniture, dishes and whatever. Grandpa (Phil & Kate Lynch) said they were going to go to Grand Island and retire and go to the doctors. He was a nice old guy and we would read old World Heralds and magazines by the hour to him. The tragedy with him was that the radio was broken. Grandma said I probably couldn't go to high school as there wasn't any money. But they left in August '37 and we never did see them again. It was better with them gone and we could use the kitchen.

Mom went to the bank and borrowed money. I was to stay and Mrs. McDermott's in Oconto for \$2.50 a week and go to 9th grade. Peg walked 3 miles to the country school.

The sewing machine didn't work, so Mom made me 2 dresses by hand. At McDermott's, I wash out underwear and socks but I had fun. Had to take geometry, they alternated geometry and algebra. Every evening the kids gathered up on main street until dark. Their radio only went on to hear Lyle Bremser and the news. I got acquainted real fast and enjoyed all the small town activities.

Things were not getting any better at the farm. Before Christmas, Dad has his pleurisy again and wasn't well. Mom wrote her brother Jack who lived in Paxton, NE if he could come get Peg and me. The day after Christmas he arrived, we loaded up our belongings and went to Paxton.

Page 8

Mary, Jack's wife was a relatively new bride. Peg's brothers Bill and Jim had come from the orphanage to live with Jack and Mary. The first thing they did was buy us some new clothes. I slept on the couch in the parlor. Mary made a huge pink angel food [cake] for my birthday. Jim was 15, Bill and I were 14 and Peg was 13 and we could keep things moving. I got to go to wedding dances in Paxton and Oles' Bar was off limits. I could always make people laugh and Jack thought I should be a standup comic and imitate Lazer Pitts. There was more food there than I had seen in a long time. The day after school was out Jack took us back to Hastings.

I don't know how but Mom drove Dad to Hastings to see the Dr and she moved furniture out of the upstairs bedroom back to their original places.

Dad's pleurisy turned out to be heart problems and he was to take it easy. He had gotten hired back as Supt. In Heartwell in the fall. So all was well again. We had moved 4 times in less than 2 years. Gave us a lot of good experience when nothing seemed to go right.

I can write a lot more before and after and during these years. Things were really tense between Grandma and Grandpa in Oconto, however all was great when we came home from Paxton and next March twins were born that died at birth. So to be continued.

Love and prayers,
Grandma Patsy